Drone Warfare

War and Conflict in the Modern World

Drone Warfare

JOHN KAAG AND SARAH KREPS

polity

First published in 2014 by Polity Press

Polity Press
65 Bridge Street
Cambridge CB2 1UR, UK

Polity Press
350 Main Street
Malden, MA 02148, USA

ISBN-13: 978-0-7456-8098-9
ISBN-13: 978-0-7456-8099-6(pb)

A catalogue record for this book is available from the British Library.

Typeset in 10.25 on 13 pt Scala by
Servis Filmsetting Ltd, Stockport, Cheshire
Printed and bound in Great Britain by T.J. International, Padstow, Cornwall

For further information on Polity, visit our website: www.politybooks.com

Contents

Tables and Figures

Preface

In writing *Drone Warfare*, we hope to provide a comprehensive, timely, rigorous, accessible analysis of the use of combat drones in modern warfare. The book's comprehensiveness required two scholars from very different fields – philosophy and political science – to work together on a single study. Its timeliness depended on working together quickly and carefully to identify the political, legal, and moral implications of this transformational technology. Its rigor meant that shortcuts were to be avoided. Its accessibility meant that certain shortcuts had to be taken.

In short, the writing of the book was immensely frustrating. So an obvious question remains: why did we endure this frustration?

For the last ten years, we watched, with growing alarm, a shift in military affairs that was defined by the use of semi-autonomous weapon systems. Our alarm was elicited not by the technology itself, but by the way that the research and development of this technology outpaced the studied consideration of its implications. These implications had nothing to do with technology and everything to do with human beings: the human beings using these unmanned technologies in asymmetric warfare and the human beings being targeted or harmed by them. In our machine era, it is tempting to think that difficult human judgments – political, legal, and moral – can be farmed out to bots that can do a better job than us. We should resist this temptation. *Drone Warfare* is a reminder that human judgment will be an inescapable part of the drone age. While it is necessary to understand how drones are currently used (as outlined in chapter 2), it is even more important to get a handle on the way that they should be used in the future. And this is why we happily faced the frustration of writing the rest of the book.

In truth, there are many other reasons that this book finally came to press and they have nothing to do with its authors. Much of what is elegant and accurate about this volume can be credited to a large number of individuals who assisted with the editing and revision of its various parts. We would like to thank David Blair, Robert Chesney, Neta Crawford, Janina Dill, Matthew Evangelista, Gustavo Flores-Macías, Carol Hay, Peter Katzenstein, Mary Ellen O'Connell, David O'Hara, Jens Ohlin, Capt. Bill Parker, Scott Pratt, Klem Ryan, Judith Reppy, Bassam Romaya, Henry Shue, Colonel Rob Spalding, Geoff Wallace, Matthew Waxman, Micah Zenko, and, not least, we thank Kyle Ezzedine and Rebecca Friedman for valuable research assistance. We would especially like to thank Whitley Kaufman for his help in revising chapters 4 and 5 of the book.

In the case of Kaag's contribution to this volume, much of the research was accomplished during a fellowship at the American Academy of Arts and Sciences. Kreps completed the manuscript while she was a fellow at the Council on Foreign Relations in New York. Members of these organizations have given daily feedback and encouragement in the course of the project.

Drone Warfare is the product of a long-standing collaboration between its authors. The ideas presented in this volume were first hatched in a number of articles in both peer-reviewed and public venues. This book presented us with the opportunity to unify our arguments into a single cohesive narrative about the reality and future of drone warfare. We are pragmatists and as pragmatists we believe that theory needs to impact practice. Writing for a wider public is not ancillary to our work as scholars, and short, self-contained articles are often the one way to effect real-world change. In many cases, our public writings on drone warfare have had real and immediate traction in policy debates. This being said, each argument, presented over the course of nearly four years, has been situated in a broader, systematic treatment of drones. In addition to presenting new arguments concerning drones, this volume gave us the opportunity to explain the way that our previous work on the subject over the last four years fits together and it is greater than the sum of its parts.

Practical, systematic, careful thinking is what is needed when it comes to drone warfare. At this point, we do not need better weapon systems. We need better judgment in using the ones at our disposal. There is a complex relationship between the politics, the law, and the morality of drone strikes and it is a relationship that remains largely overlooked in the current debates about modern asymmetric warfare. Understanding this relationship will not be easy. It will require consulting experts who seem to have nothing to do with military tactics: political theorists, applied psychologists, legal theorists, and the occasional ethicist. *Drone Warfare* is an initial attempt to begin this difficult debate.

CHAPTER ONE

Introduction:
The Rise of Drones

In October 2009, then-Secretary of State Hillary Clinton traveled to Pakistan in support of the Obama Administration's efforts to convince Islamabad to crack down on terrorists.[1] A day before her arrival, however, a US drone strike killed more than one hundred Pakistanis in that country's tribal region. Thus, when Clinton stood in front of a press conference in Islamabad, she faced two questions that inverted the very premise of her trip. First, Clinton was asked to define terrorism. Then came the follow-up: "Is it [terrorism] the killing of people in drone attacks?"[2] That question – volleyed by a woman from the back of the audience – perfectly encapsulates the moral, legal, and political ambiguities that prompted us to write this book.

Of course, Clinton's response was as simple as it was emphatic: No, drone strikes are not acts of terrorism. The Obama Administration's spokesperson Jay Carney recently stated even more clearly: "Drone strikes are legal, they are ethical, and they are wise."[3] But as unmanned aerial vehicles (UAVs), drones are qualitatively different than previous military technologies: they allow lethal action at virtually no risk to the perpetrator. As such, it is a mistake to take their legality, morality, and prudence for granted. This book seeks neither to excoriate nor to vindicate contemporary drone policy. Instead, we examine the political, legal, and moral dimensions of the policy and provide a synthetic assessment of the dangers of its current trajectory.

Drones represent the intersection of two important trends in military technology: the increasingly precise nature of weapons and the rise of robotics. Taken together, these ever-more-sophisticated capabilities produced a drone aircraft, flown remotely at no risk to the pilot and capable of delivering a lethal payload. On the surface, drone technology seems to offer great benefits: it allows the United States to take the fight to terrorists, wherever they may hide, without risking the lives of American service members. Often lost in that seductive proposition, however, are the second-order effects created by this capability. It is precisely the novelty of drone capabilities that creates new challenges.

Our engagement with US drone policy turns on three mutually supportive pillars: politics, law, and morality. Politically, the costs of war are no longer distributed throughout a democratic society; thus, the costliness of war in blood and treasure, which has historically reined in military adventurism, is greatly diminished. We worry that this dynamic risks enabling a state of perpetual, low-level conflict underneath the public's radar. Legally, drones seem to alleviate confusion over important points of international law, such as distinction and proportionality, but this appearance only further entrenches dangerous ambiguities. Indeed, the legal edifice supporting the United States' drone policy goes beyond reasonable interpretation of the principles of *jus ad bellum* as well as *jus in bello* by expanding the battlefield to include individuals and spaces considered outside legally recognized combat zones. Morally, drones create a "moral hazard" by shielding US citizens, politicians, and soldiers from the risks associated with targeted killings; unfortunately, these same individuals lack the ethical training to consider the normative dangers of drones. Consequently, drones are becoming banal – leaving their ethical implications unexamined and their ease of use celebrated as intrinsically good. Cumulatively, these arguments comprise a call to action, not necessarily to resist drones as an instrument of warfare, but rather to employ them only if the international community is cognizant of, and comfortable with, their manifold implications.

As the title suggests, this is a book about drones. We take drones as our subject because we believe that the speed of technological development in this area has far outpaced our understanding of how that technology interacts with politics, international law, and ethics. This is not a book about the evolution of airpower, or weapons technology, over time. Consequently, our reservations about drones are not tantamount to endorsements of previous, less precise technologies like carpet-bombing. We see the US military's commitment to minimize civilian casualties as an unequivocally positive development.[4] Rather, we seek to elucidate ongoing debates about drone policy by emphasizing, for example, that even a technology that makes discrimination between civilians and combatants easier does not obviate the problem of discrimination, and that minimizing risks to American pilots may save lives in the short term but it also undermines the accountability linkages that keep wars short and bounded in the long term. Moreover, while accepting the tactical effectiveness of drones, we contend that they are not strategically effective – suggesting that there are practical as well as normative reasons to question extant drone policy. Consistent with our pragmatic approach, after exploring the complexities of drones throughout the book, we conclude with recommendations for how drones policy can change to allay some of our normative concerns.

The turn to drones

The use of drones in combat has increased considerably over the last decade. Having authorized just nine strikes outside the context of combat between 2004 and 2007, the Bush Administration authorized thirty-six such strikes in its last year of office. President Obama dramatically increased the use of drones, primarily in the tribal regions of Pakistan and to a lesser extent in Yemen and Somalia. Between 2009 and 2012, there were 295 strikes in Pakistan alone, resulting in about 2,221 casualties, of which about 1,800 were suspected militants, 153 were civilians, and 205 were of unknown identity. While the rate of strikes in Pakistan has declined from its peak in 2010, the number in Yemen has increased, as the United States battles the increasingly powerful al-Qaeda in the Arabian Peninsula.[5] The United States has also conducted a handful of drone strikes in Somalia against al-Shabab, an al-Qaeda affiliate.[6]

As recently as the 1990s, drones were not armed at all. They took the form of sensor aircraft, with Predators operating in Bosnia, Kosovo, and the no-fly zone in Iraq.[7] Inevitably, however, debates about combat capability arose. Whereas the air force demanded fast, "jet-like" drones, the CIA preferred smaller, surveillance drones. Both the air force and the CIA expressed interest in going beyond gathering intelligence and acquiring an aircraft that could both track and kill suspected targets, although there was considerable debate about how or whether to do so. At the time, CIA Counterterrorist Center Director Cofer Black argued that the United States should not deploy Predators over Afghanistan until they were weaponized, saying "I do not believe the possible recon value outweighs the risk of possible program termination when the stakes are raised by the Taliban parading a charred Predator in front of CNN."[8] Yet the armed version of the Predator also had its dissenters prior to 9/11. Former CIA Director George Tenet suggested that it would be "a terrible mistake" for "the Director of Central Intelligence to fire a weapon like this."[9]

After 9/11, the "gloves came off" and the CIA sent Predators to Afghanistan on September 16, and armed Predators followed on October 7.[10] It was in the post-9/11 threat environment that the United States began undertaking targeted killings by drones, deploying the MQ-1B Predator and the MQ-9 Reaper, armed with precision-guided munitions, to match their adversaries' flexible tactics. The first CIA drone attack occurred in November 2001, when a Predator killed Mohammed Atef, the "number three" in al-Qaeda.[11] A year later, on November 4, 2002, the Agency launched an attack in Yemen, its "first targeted killing outside of a declared war zone using the 'sweeping authority' given to the spy agency by Bush in September 2001."[12] The target was al-Harethi, the terrorist leader responsible for the *USS Cole* bombing. Yemeni President Saleh claimed responsibility for the attack on al-Harethi, but, after it was leaked that the United States was behind the strike, drones were not used in the country until 2009. However, in 2004, because of the rise of the Pakistani Taliban and the failure of the Pakistani military, the CIA was granted access to conduct surveillance and targeted killing across Pakistan's Federally Administered Tribal Areas. It has since conducted hundreds of such strikes.[13] The government claims to have approximately 7,500 drones, up from just a few dozen a decade ago.[14]

Thus, what began as an engineering experiment to fit Hellfire missiles onto a surveillance drone in 2001 has turned into a transformation of how the United States uses military force, and, by many accounts, a tactically successful one. Even those who question whether the strategy is effective – wondering whether the use of drones is ultimately recruiting more terrorists than it kills – concede that the use of drones has eliminated key al-Qaeda leaders.[15] Underlining the basis for drones is that the drone policy makes for good domestic politics. The United States has killed leaders of al-Qaeda and its affiliates while reducing its own casualties and reducing the domestic blowback that comes from body bags returning from war. To the extent that increased casualties reduce the popularity of a conflict and in turn reduce a leader's strategic options,[16] drones have given leaders greater freedom of action to carry out wars without domestic scrutiny or meaningful constraints.

Indeed, poll data suggest that the American public is widely accepting – while at the same time somewhat ignorant – of US drone strikes abroad. A large majority (65 percent) of Americans claim that they have heard a lot about the US drone program, but when asked where most strikes are occurring, most Americans either cite the wrong country or do not know where those strikes are carried out.[17] More broadly, an astounding majority of people (75 percent) report that they nevertheless approve of these targeting practices, even though their knowledge of the policy is dubious.[18] Yet, in the very same poll, only a quarter of respondents aver that drone strikes are legal.

One thing is clear from the politics surrounding the drone program: Americans express significantly greater concern about drone strikes when the policy seems to affect them directly. As we suggest in chapter 3, Americans are more agitated about the prospect of being spied on by drones than they are by the targeting of individuals in other countries. Moreover, the revelation that the US government has used drones to kill its own citizens and under some circumstances would be willing to do so again in the future caused a public outcry. By bringing the drone issue "home," an impression furthered by substantial media and Congressional attention to the possibility of lethal drone strikes on US soil, the program finally captured the public imagination. Indeed, out of more than three thousand casualties resulting from US drone strikes,[19] the killing of four Americans dominated the 2013 nomination hearings for CIA Director John Brennan. Despite the increased public attention, most of the populace remains ill-equipped to explain the basic "when and where" of drone strikes as they currently take place.

We should note from the outset that, while this is a book about drones, it tends to focus on the use of drones by the United States. The United States has been the country to conduct the most drone strikes – far more than either Israel or the United Kingdom – providing a useful case study into how drones are used, the domestic politics around the use of drones by a democracy, and the diplomatic consequences of their use. This case study also provides insight into how domestic politics might affect the interpretation of international law and the way that this interpretation might not coincide with some basic ethical arguments that underpin modern liberal societies. It is with this case-study approach in mind that many of the examples we cite feature the United States, but we suspect that they are likely instructive in terms of other countries using drones, especially democracies where the domestic imperatives of minimizing casualties may be especially salient. We do, however, highlight the proliferation of drones internationally. While just forty-one countries had drones in 2005, that number had increased to seventy-six by 2011.[20] Most of these are not combat drones, but every major regional actor – friend and foe alike – has either combat drones or plans to acquire them. The second and concluding chapters review the proliferation trends and propose measures to deal respectively with the control and regulation of drone use.

Existing accounts of drone warfare

Prior to 1980, drone warfare was largely the province of science fiction such as Frank Herbert's *Dune* (1965) and Isaac Asimov's Robot series.[21] The first books to discuss it as a reality typically addressed the practical and technical challenges that faced designers and engineers. The second wave of drone literature began to provide instructions on how best to use these new devices in a variety of military theaters. "Best" in this sense simply referred to the practical questions of efficiency and strategic advantage. Peter Singer's *Wired for War* (2009) may not have been the first but it became the most popular book-length treatment of unmanned aerial vehicles. Singer, for the most part, avoids the theoretical work that we take up in the coming chapters and concentrates his energies on providing a comprehensive analysis of the design, capabilities, and strategy of unmanned aerial vehicles. In other words, Singer concentrates on bringing together the insights of the first two waves of drone literature, and he does this very effectively. He briefly addresses the impact that drones will have on political processes and international law, but, for the most part, questions concerning the legal, political, and moral implications of drones and other semiautonomous weapon systems are generally left for another day. That day has come and we are faced with the rather difficult task of thinking through the implications of a technology that is being implemented at unprecedented speed.

The capabilities of these new technologies have radically expanded in the last decade, and scholars of warfare have struggled to keep up. As Micah Zenko writes:

> Five-pound backpack drones are now used by infantry soldiers for tactical surveillance and will soon be deployed for what their manufacture calls "magic bullet" kamikaze missions. Special operations forces have developed a warhead fired from a Predator drone that can knock down doors. K-Max helicopter drones transport supplies to troops at forward operating bases in Afghanistan. Balloons unleash Tempest drones, which then send out smaller surveillance

drones – called Cicadas – that glide to the ground to collect data. And now the US State Department is flying a small fleet of surveillance drones over Iraq to protect the US Embassy there. Bottom line: More and more drones have been rushed into service, and their use and application by the US military is seemingly infinite.[22]

As the technology has expanded, a growing number of books, primarily anthologies, have taken on the normative implications of drone technologies. Theorists – legal, political, and moral – often find themselves scrambling to explain, defend, and criticize technologies that have already been developed, and, in most cases, have already been used. This "shoot first and ask questions later" mentality recurs in the history of modern military technology. For example, in 1954, President Harry Truman pleaded with an international community that was just beginning to witness an unprecedented nuclear arms race: "We must catch up morally and internationally with the machine age. We must catch up with it, and we must catch up with it in such a way as to create peace in the world, or it will destroy us and everybody else. And that we don't dare to contemplate."[23]

The danger of technology outpacing well-reasoned scholarship is as present in the age of drone warfare as it was in the age of thermonuclear weapons. Journalists and experts in international law, political science, and moral theory have each made a run at catching up with this potentially transformational military technology.[24] But recent attempts have only been partially successful because they have hewn too closely to disciplinary divides. Save for the fact that multidisciplinary arguments appeared in the same anthologies, it has remained unclear how the legal, political, and moral arguments concerning drones are interrelated. We maintain that they are inextricable and only an account of unmanned aerial systems that takes seriously the relationship between politics, law, and morality will be rich enough to address the complexities of our drone age adequately. In this respect, the division of the book into three discrete sections – politics, law, and morality – is an artificial one that is analytically useful but potentially misleading. Ultimately, our argument is synthetic and interdisciplinary, reflecting the fact that in the real world, where individuals face the effects of drone warfare with bone-jarring clarity, such distinctions lack relevance.

This volume, co-authored by a political scientist and a philosopher, undertakes a unified moral reckoning of combat drone technologies, but does so with a mind to the political, legal, and ethical realities that define modern international relations. The scope of our book, however, is limited to the use of unmanned aerial vehicles in military strikes, and more specifically to targeted killings. We address the issue of UAV intelligence, surveillance, and reconnaissance only tangentially. Most military drones are not directly involved in targeted killings, but in this book we do not address the question of UAVs for nonlethal missions, both domestic and international, which present qualitatively different challenges. Instead, we focus on the way that combat drones stand to transform how wars are fought, and, perhaps more importantly, on the way that we understand the very definitions of war and peace. How exactly do drones change military strategy or the ethics of war and peace? Does a drone strike constitute an act of war? Does the use of drones make war more or less likely? What standards – political, legal, and ethical – might effectively limit their use? Should there even be a limit? As strategists, policy makers, and scholars begin to think through the use of these pivotal technologies, they will need to answer these questions.

Confronting "dirty hands"

This book explicates how the speed of drone technologies out-strips our understanding of their implications for politics, law, and moral theory. There are, we believe, two reasons for this: the rapid pace of technological advancement, and widespread faith in technological "progress." First, modern technologi-cal life is always in process – research and development is currently generating new technological innovations – so achieving intellectual mastery of technology is an ever-elusive goal. From this perspective, this book is a project of theoretical catch-up. As such, it explores the normatively charged emer-gence of drones within a particular constellation of economic interests, geopolitical concerns, legal norms, and ethical ideals. The value-laden background conditions of today's technologies, and specifically drones, however, are often overlooked in their rapid developmental stages. Part of theo-retical catch-up involves going back – looking at the reasons why drones have increased and how they have been used. However, the ultimate objective is to move forward. The fun-damental aim of this book is to inform a reader of the most pivotal issues in the coming drone debate. How do leading countries set up systems in which drones proliferated? What should the rules of the road look like for the use of drones? What is the legal or institutional vehicle by which these rules operate? We hope that scholars, politicians, military planners, and most importantly, citizens will be part of this debate. If this is going to happen, there is some catching up to do.

The second reason why our technological capabilities outpace our understanding of them is the widespread belief that tech-nological advancement is itself synonymous with "progress" and therefore does not need to be regulated. Simply put, it is the assumption that technological advancement is *necessarily* good. This is a dangerous assumption. On this note, we agree, in principle, with former legal advisor to the State Department Harold Koh that "advanced technologies have helped to make our targeting more precise." We, however, would observe that this statement is far from complete (since advanced technologies could in fact be used in highly questionable targeting practices), and we suggest that technological precision should not be conflated with choices that are legal or ethical, even if they offer sound political options for electoral-minded leaders. In particular, the questions of where and whom we target are inherently fraught, complicated by subjective views of combatant status, for example. We should not be seduced into thinking that technology can help us out of these legal and ethical dilemmas. In many cases, greater technological capability coincides with a greater difficulty in making responsible decisions. Our main worry is that the US government's attempts to neutralize terrorist threats may reproduce the very tactics that we find most objectionable about these non-state actors whereby: our goal of satisfying one norm of just war theory stands to vitiate others; liberal democracies develop technologies that insulate their citizens from harm but in doing so they may undercut democracy itself; and our rhetoric about being free and being just may allow us to be anything but.

This last concern raises the problem of "dirty hands" – an issue that philosophers since Machiavelli have discussed with increasing urgency. Most famously in the contemporary era, Michael Walzer articulates the idea that the correct political action might involve the violation of particular moral and legal norms in extreme situations; hence a political leader must, in certain extreme cases, "dirty" his or her hands in order to avoid certain disastrous outcomes. We are not naive about this moral and practical difficulty. While we suspect that increasingly dirty hands will define our age of international terrorism, there are three salient questions that we must ask about these moral dilemmas.[25]

The first is one of degree and probability: how grave and how likely must the risks to a citizenry be in order for a leader to adopt a policy such as targeted killing? When Walzer formulated the problem in the 1970s, he suggested that moral wrongdoing (such as torture or causing the death of a limited number of innocent civilians) might be the appropriate action in cases where hundreds of innocent people could be spared in the process. Since then, he has suggested that the threat must be even starker and jeopardize an entire people or a way of life.[26]

The second question concerning "dirty hands" is about whether the morally dubious action is actually effective in neutralizing the threat. If the "dirtying" action is not effective in bringing about the desired result, it is quite obvious that it would be morally *and* politically impermissible. We will address both the immediate and long-term effectiveness of targeted killing in the early chapters of this book.

Finally, there is the question of how we are to describe the moral and legal dirt that accumulates on the hands of leaders who turn to drone technologies in targeted killings. Surely this moral messiness should not be swept under the political carpet by blandly asserting that such strikes are "legal, ethical, and wise." They aren't, at least in any unproblematic way. Perhaps they are a necessary evil, but part of this book is meant to determine how necessary and how evil.

Behind the advancement of drone technology over the last decade is also the unspoken belief that the values and liberties of modern democracy are worth defending and that the populace is averse to expending the lives of its own citizen soldiers in the process. This belief surfaces when the drone debate hits too close to home, when politicians and citizens object to the idea of targeting American citizens and to the mere prospect of domestic drone surveillance. This protest against certain drone capabilities indicates that democratic values *are* still worth protecting. But if this is the case, then the rest of the drone program – the part that involves targeting foreign nationals without transparency or adequate oversight – needs to be assessed carefully and critically in order to see whether it compromises the political, legal, and ethical foundations upon which liberal democracies are grounded. This is not an age of simple answers.

Outline

This book proceeds in six chapters. Following the introduction, the second chapter presents a "nuts and bolts" discussion of what drones are, what they do, and the growing prevalence of drones, particularly in the context of the "war on terror." As we show through data for drone strikes over the last decade, these strikes have increased considerably, with more strikes used for the purposes of counterterrorism in President Obama's first term than in the entire Bush Administration.[27] We outline the intragovernmental decision-making process that produces drone strikes, particularly questions of agency jurisdiction, targeting decisions, and transparency. In this chapter, we also preview the state of proliferation: which countries are acquiring drones and which already have drones in their arsenals. We also assess the military effectiveness of drones. Individuals such as former Defense Secretary Leon Panetta have said that drones are "the only game in town."[28] To be sure, drones offer a low-risk way to decapitate terrorist organizations, but they also create visceral opposition that lends itself to recruiting new terrorists. We explore that dynamic – the long-term adverse strategic consequences versus the short-term tactical gains – in chapter 2.

Having set the stage for our analysis of drone warfare, we turn to the political, legal, and ethical implications of drones in military operations. In addressing these implications, we gesture toward a particular relationship between politics, law – both domestic and international – and morality. Politics, at its most basic, is a social organization whereby individuals pursue interests and secure resources that they could not pursue or secure independently. This is at the core of all modern social contracts that underpin the majority of today's states. Politics, in turn, provides the normative force to laws, both domestic and international. Laws require a certain amount of "buy-in" by political leaders and administrators in order to be practically legitimate. Of course, domestic, constitutional law can influence the shape of politics once this "buy-in" occurs, but this is less often the case with international law that tends not to be as binding as constitutional law on political processes. The case of unmanned aerial systems demonstrates this clearly to the extent that their domestic use for surveillance has been met with a firestorm of opposition from the US public on the basis of constitutional concerns, but their use internationally has not generated similar concerns on the basis of international law. The place of ethics in this discussion is a difficult one to define and is often left out of analyses of drone warfare. Ideally, the interpretation and execution of laws reflect what is regarded as moral conduct in a given culture within the context of a given polity. Ethical reflection is required in cases where the interpretation and execution of laws is out of sync with moral intuitions, and, more specifically, with the moral arguments that have purchase in a given culture. (We can see this in the case of the Jim Crow laws and the ethical appeal of the civil rights movement.) We offer a selection of moral arguments that stand to affect the use of combat drones within the current legal and political setting.

In the third chapter, on politics, we turn our attention to the way that the drones debate has played out in the US political sphere and suggest that certain forms of drone warfare have compromised democratic accountability. Rather than turning our attention from international politics, this focus underscores the way that public opinion in the domestic sphere might impact foreign policy, including the issue of drone strikes. Beginning with Kant in 1795, many scholars in international relations have embraced the idea that republics, and by extension modern democracies, will restrain how leaders use military force due to the costs that war imposes on an electorate. Leaders will be unwilling to put citizens in harm's way if these citizens are responsible for their maintenance of power. But what happens when technologies such as drones are used to shield soldiers from harm while nonetheless engaging in military campaigns? We suggest that the use of drones shields the public from the consequences and costs of war, which prevents the public backlash that restrains leaders from conducting wars. The world becomes a global battlefield in both time and space. The chapter underscores a dangerous irony about democratic peace theory: citizens want to be protected and therefore encourage their elected governments to develop technologies that will reduce the costs of war in blood and money, and drones have played this part very nicely by limiting troop involvement in campaigns since the invasion of Iraq ten years ago. However, shielding citizens from the costs of war potentially decouples the democratic process whereby leaders must seek public approval for military campaigns. Such dynamics risk introducing a state of perpetual war.

Chapter 4 turns its attention to international law. There are two main components of the legal critique of drone use in combat. The first is a critique that the use of drones in places such as Pakistan, Yemen, and Somalia violates *jus ad bellum* – the recourse to war – since the United States is not at war with any of these states but rather a non-state (al-Qaeda) within these territories. The second is a critique that the use of drones potentially violates *jus in bello*, law governing conduct in war, because the use of these technologies invites policy makers and military strategists to overstep principles of distinction and proportionality. At the same time, drone technology makes principles of distinction and proportionality much more important because it enables modern militaries to accurately strike targets from a distance – eliminating the risk of troop casualties inherent in military conflicts of the past. We examine both of these critiques as well as the counter-arguments, namely the sets of legal defenses that the Obama Administration has adduced to justify the use of drones in combat.

Chapter 5 deals with the ethics of using unmanned aerial vehicles to target suspected terrorists. Ethics provides the foundation upon which most legal and political principles, which govern the use of drones, rest. In this chapter, we show that the use of drones creates a "moral hazard," in which countries that employ drones have an incentive to undertake the risky behavior of targeted killing because technology shields them from most of the adverse consequences. The lack of ethical training for soldiers and policy makers exacerbates the moral hazard because the practical benefits of drones seem so great whereas the costs of drones, which generally function on a normative level, seem so low. This circumstance creates a danger that targeted killings will become banal – particularly if citizens accept this policy as commonplace. Finally, we build on previous chapters' discussions of civilian casualties and democratic accountability to disagree with recent philosophical works that defend drones as not only effective but morally obligatory.

In the concluding chapter of the book, we highlight the unprecedented strategic choices that the United States currently faces with its drone capabilities. We argue that this historical moment is analogous to the military and political hegemony that the United States enjoyed after World War II. At that time, the United States willingly limited its power through a web of international agreements, and eventually, arms treaties. We propose that a similar set of actions could be taken with regard to the use of drones, with the United States setting standards through its behavior on the legitimate use of drones, one that is more restrained but also more transparent in terms of the compatibility between targeting decisions and its ethical and legal commitments. We also offer policy recommendations dealing with Congressional oversight, UAV exports to other countries, and the threat that other countries with drone technologies pose to the United States. We close with speculation about the future of conflict in the age of drones.

CHAPTER TWO

The Nuts and Bolts of Drones

In November 2001, just weeks into the Afghanistan campaign, the United States undertook the first recorded use of
a drone in combat, when a Predator killed Mohammed Atef,
an al-Qaeda military commander in Afghanistan.[1] Only a year
later, the United States conducted the first drone attack outside an area of armed conflict: in November 2002, the Central
Intelligence Agency guided a Predator armed with Hellfire
missiles over Yemen to strike and kill six suspected al-Qaeda
members. The victims included Ali Qaed Senyan Al-Harethi,
who had been associated with the attack on the *USS Cole* in
2000.[2] After the Yemeni strike, the CIA paused its drone
strikes until 2004, when the United States struck al-Qaeda
and Taliban associate Nek Muhammad Wazir in Northwest
Pakistan. In these early years, the use of armed drones outside an armed conflict such as Afghanistan was episodic. By
the end of the decade, however, the use of armed drones had
become a central feature of US counterterrorism strategy,
with eighty more strikes in Yemen, more than three hundred
in Pakistan, about a dozen in Somalia, not to mention the less
controversial but frequent use of drones to strike suspected
terrorists in Afghanistan. Indeed, in a May 2013 speech,
President Obama confessed that he had come "to view drone
strikes as a cure-all for terrorism."[3]

   This chapter gives more detail on how drones have been
used in combat in order to ground the subsequent discussion about the politics, law, and ethics of drones. It examines

the technology itself, the circumstances under which drones have been used, how combat drones are proliferating in other countries, and the question of whether that technology works both strategically and tactically.

As with the book more generally, the focus of the chapter tends to be the United States, which has been the most prodigious developer and user of drones in combat. However, the chapter paints a picture of the global drone demand by way of foreshadowing the proliferation challenges we will take up in the concluding chapter. In particular, we suggest that many countries have learned the lessons of the United States: that drones offer a way to conduct military strikes while reducing risks to one's own pilots, a domestic political coup for leaders.

While we acknowledge that drone strikes have worked tactically by killing leaders of al-Qaeda, the strategic consequences are more dubious, with much evidence to suggest that the longer-term picture is complicated by questions of whether drone strikes are creating "martyrdom effects," a rallying cry for recruitment that ultimately will create an environment hostile to counterterrorism goals. However, in a preview of the politics chapter, we acknowledge that a democratic leader's time horizon is much shorter than this. Politicians hope to prevent a terrorist attack on their watch and can leave the strategic uncertainty to their successor. The subsequent chapter on politics unpacks those political dynamics – especially in terms of the checks and balances on executive authority – in more detail.

The technology

Before proceeding with a discussion of the technology, a brief word about nomenclature is perhaps in order. Until this point in the manuscript, we have generally used the term "drone" in reference to unmanned aerial vehicles but we acknowledge that this label may seem pejorative. Indeed, the United States military, and in particular the air force, prefers either unmanned aerial systems (UAS), which comprise "not only the aerial vehicle but also the ground control station, the human operators, and the mobile containers used to transport the UAVs and ground equipment." A UAS unit generally consists of more than one UAV; for example, a US air force Predator unit contains four UAVs.[4] The US military also uses remotely piloted aircraft (RPA), in part for political reasons: to put the "pilot" back into the label, correcting the impression that the aircraft is a mindless machine that performs functions without human intervention or that the human intervention behind the functions is mindless. Instead, the intention of the move away from the term "drone" is to credit the pilots with the enormous amount of training and authority they receive in piloting the aircraft and to be more accurate in referencing the humans that are behind decisions about where to orient the aircraft and what to strike.[5] For the purposes of this book, we typically use the label "drone" because we believe it is more accessible to the typical reader than either UAS or RPA. We acknowledge the technical shortcomings and wish to be clear that we do not attach any normative judgment to the term.

Drones, as these definitions imply, are remotely piloted, in other words, flown without an onboard pilot. This designation includes a number of different types of aircraft, from do-it-yourself drones that one can buy on the internet to drones used for the purposes of domestic surveillance to combat drones used in military strikes, with a number of varieties in between.[6] According to the Government Accountability Office (GAO), fifty countries are in the process of developing 900 UAVs.[7] Our analysis generally focuses on armed drones. We suggest that, by virtue of using military force, these are qualitatively different from other types of drones, even surveillance drones, which have their share of critics. The technical discussion below is weighted toward armed drones in order to situate the substantive chapters on domestic politics, international law, and ethics that follow.

Drones are generally differentiated along several parameters, including function, size, payload, geographical range, flight endurance, and altitude. The payload refers to the carrying capacity of the aircraft, including the contents and potential weight of cargo (if any). Geographical range, flight endurance, and maximum ceiling are the maximum distance, time, and altitude that drones can reach during an interrupted mission. Drones are classified as different types, depending on where they lie along these parameters. The US air force, the most prolific operator of drones, classifies its drones into five tiers, which are distinguished by altitude and function; the other services have fewer tiers and all essentially map onto the air force tier system, albeit with less granularity. Tier N/A refers to small and micro UAVs with a range of five miles, an endurance of an hour, and a ceiling of 1,000 feet. Tier 1 refers to low-altitude and long-endurance aircraft, covering the low-altitude layer of about 30,000 ft. Tier 2 contains medium-altitude, long-endurance drones and extends to an altitude of 50,000 ft, which contains the troposphere. The MQ-1 Predator and the MQ-9 Reaper are both classified as Tier 2 UAVs. Tier 2+ are high-altitude, long-endurance UAVs that reach 70,000 ft (such as the RQ-4 Global Hawk), and are complemented by Tier 3–, which are high-altitude stealth UAVs, none of which have been produced.[8]

This classification system generally maps onto a more general approach, which is to designate by altitude and endurance. For example, there are also high-altitude long-endurance drones, typically surveillance aircraft such as the Global Hawk.[9] More germane to this analysis are the medium-altitude and long-endurance, or "MALE," drones, which generally correspond to Tier 2 drones: the MALE drones are seen to be desirable in that they are less vulnerable to light anti-aircraft[10] but still have a respectable endurance. Long endurance is desirable insofar as the ability to loiter and operate for long periods is one of the key virtues of a drone: it does not have to deal with the human limitations that apply to manned aircraft. Longer endurance also means a lower "manpower burden and operating cost" due to fewer takeoffs and landings.[11]

Of these so-called MALE drones, the most frequently employed, at least by the United States – and therefore as a proportion of total strikes in the annals of drone history – have been the MQ-1B Predator and the MQ-9 Reaper. Table 2.1 compares the key characteristics of both aircraft. Both are capable of surveillance and attack, although the Predator

Table 2.1 Key features of Predator and Reaper drones		
	MQ-1B Predator	**MQ-9 Reaper**
Primary function:	Armed reconnaissance, airborne surveillance and target acquisition	Remotely piloted hunter/killer weapon system
Wingspan:	55 feet (16.8 meters)	66 feet (20.1 meters)
Length:	27 feet (8.22 meters)	36 feet (11 meters)
Height:	6.9 feet (2.1 meters)	12.5 feet (3.8 meters)
Payload:	3,850 lb (1,746 kg)	3,750 pounds (1,701 kg)
Range:	Up to 770 miles (675 nautical miles)	1,150 miles (1,000 nautical miles)
Max Endurance:	27 hours	14 hours (fully loaded)
Max Altitude:	50,000 feet (15,240 meters)	Up to 50,000 feet (15,240 meters)
Armament:	Two laser-guided AGM-114 Hellfire missiles	Combination of AGM-114 Hellfire missiles, GBU-12 Paveway II and GBU-38 Joint Direct Attack Munitions

Sources: United States Air Force and General Atomics Aeronautical fact sheets, MQ-1B-Predator and MQ-9-Reaper

specializes in surveillance while the Reaper specializes in combat. The Predator can be equipped with two laser-guided Hellfire missiles, has an operating speed of between 84 mph and 135 mph, a range of 770 miles, a flight endurance of 24 hours, and a maximum ceiling of 25,000 feet. It serves the "killer/scout role as an intelligence collection asset and secondarily against dynamic execution targets." The Predator also operates with a multi-spectral targeting system, providing the drone's operators with real-time full-motion video at 30 frames per second.[12] As an indication of their surveillance capabilities, Predator drones have recently been employed in US domestic law enforcement, including municipal police forces, border patrol, the FBI, and the CIA. While these domestic Predator drones are unarmed, their usage has unleashed waves of privacy-related controversy.[13]

In contrast, the Reaper is faster, heavier, and more lethal than the Predator.[14] It employs a combination of Hellfire missiles, Paveway II and Joint Direct Attack Munitions, has an operating speed of around 230 mph, a geographical range of 1,150 miles, a flight endurance of 14 hours, and a maximum ceiling of 50,000 feet.[15] Because of its more limited 14-hour endurance, it is primarily employed in the "hunter/killer role against dynamic execution targets and secondarily as an intelligence collection asset."[16]

Compared to fighter jets, drones are generally less costly. They do have a higher mishap rate, about 7.6 per 100,000 flight hours for a Predator compared to 2.36 for an F-15, and technically a higher per unit cost than the F-15 and F-16, although since neither is currently being acquired by the United States, the relevant comparison is with the more modern manned aircraft that the United States is procuring.[17] The unmanned Reaper costs approximately US$20 million to produce while the fifth-generation stealth fighter, the manned F-22 Raptor, has a per unit cost of about US$185 million, and the F-35 Joint Strike Fighter about US$136 million.[18] The Raven is an even smaller and cheaper UAV, weighing in at 4.2 lbs, and costs only US$35,000 to build.[19] One exception to the cost advantage of UAVs is the Global Hawk, whose costs escalated to the point where it became unclear whether there were financial virtues to deploying it versus the U-2 predecessor.[20]

Despite their financial and tactical advantages that will be discussed later, drones suffer from two primary weaknesses. First, drones are currently not equipped for air-to-air combat. As the Chief of Air Combat Command General Hostage noted, "Predators and Reapers are useless in a contested environment . . . I couldn't put [a Predator or Reaper] into the Strait of Hormuz without having to put airplanes there to protect it."[21] Second, they are vulnerable to signal disruption and jamming. Drone technology is only effective as long as it has secure datalinks. Enemies against which the United States has used drones to date have not been especially technologically or militarily advanced. According to the Deputy Chief of Naval Operations for Warfare Systems, "through most of the decade, they [drones] have been able to operate in a permissive environment, neither congested nor contested. [In the future], frequently the environment will be physically and electronically contested," which means hacking and jamming datalinks that prevent the drones from operating effectively.[22] To circumvent vulnerability, however, will require considerable investments in drone research and development – for example anti-air and electronic warfare capabilities, flares, jammers, and decoys – that reduce a drone's financial advantage.[23]

The use of drones in combat

For most of the drone program's history, the US government ran two parallel initiatives – one covert and one publicly acknowledged. The CIA ran the secret program, overseeing the deployment of drones outside of combat zones; in other words, everywhere beside Afghanistan, Iraq, and Libya. Thus, many lethal drone strikes have occurred in Pakistan, Yemen, and Somalia as covert operations under CIA purview. These operations are authorized under Title 50, which gives the CIA the authority to complete covert operations "to influence political, economic, or military conditions abroad" without the appearance or acknowledgment of a US government role. These actions do "not include traditional military activities." As covert operations – as opposed to military operations – Title 50 activities do not require public disclosure. The second, parallel, drone program was developed under military auspices in the combat zones of Afghanistan, Iraq, and Libya. Unlike the CIA program, the military program is not covert because it is authorized under Title 10, which governs the armed forces and requires public disclosure.[24]

Drones in combat zones
While much of the media attention on drones has focused on the CIA drone strikes in places such as Pakistan and Yemen, the majority of strikes between 2008 and 2012 were actually Department of Defense strikes, especially in Afghanistan but also in Iraq and Libya when the United States was involved in conflicts in these countries. Although the government itself has reversed an earlier policy of publishing monthly updates on drone strikes in Afghanistan, meaning that official data are unavailable, groups such as the Bureau of Investigative Journalism have pieced together information. Between 2008 and 2012, there were about 1,200 coalition drone strikes in Afghanistan.

The United States was not the only country responsible for drone use, however; it appears as though the United Kingdom conducted 20–30% of these strikes, with higher strike rates as a percentage of overall sorties than the US fleet (7% com-

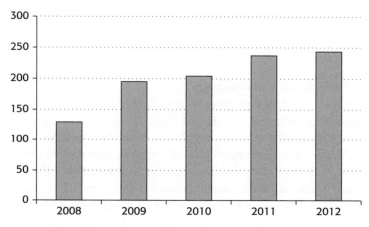

Source: Bureau of Investigative Journalism[25]

Figure 2.1 Total coalition drone strikes in Afghanistan between 2008 and 2012

pared to 2% for the United States).[26] Neither the United States nor the United Kingdom has revealed anything about casualties resulting from drone strikes in Afghanistan, keeping the information classified and, in the case of the British Ministry of Defence, suggesting that it would not collect data on casualties "because of the immense difficulty and risks that would be involved in collecting robust data." In addition to the drone strikes in Afghanistan, the United States also conducted 105 drone strikes in Libya in 2011 and 47 in Iraq.[27]

These strikes in the context of armed conflict have not been subject to the same level of scrutiny as those outside the countries where the United States has been directly at war, the tacit understanding being that military-directed strikes in the context of armed conflicts such as those in Afghanistan, Iraq, and Libya are qualitatively different than those pursued by the CIA in places like Pakistan, Yemen, and Somalia. Thus, the following sections focus on the latter strikes, including their frequency, the rate of civilian casualties, and ideas as to why they have increased in some geographic areas while decreasing in others.

Drones outside of combat zones
Outside Afghanistan, the United States has used combat drones most prevalently in Pakistan, as Figure 2.2 suggests. The first American strike in Pakistan took place in June 2004 in Waziristan, the tribal region of Pakistan where most of the drone strikes have been concentrated, and killed about seven people, four of whom were suspected militants. There were no more strikes that year. For each of the next three years, the use of drones was fairly limited although marked by a general increase. The increasing reliance on drones as a central feature of the US counterterrorism policy began in earnest in 2008 and peaked in 2009–10, as shown in Figure 2.2.

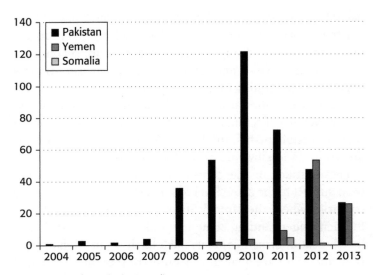

Source: Bureau of Investigative Journalism

Figure 2.2 Number of American drone strikes by country

While the total number of strikes in Pakistan increased dramatically between 2008 and 2010 (as shown in Figure 2.2), they have declined in subsequent years. In contrast, while they are fewer in total number, the prevalence of strikes elsewhere, especially in Yemen, has increased. In 2012 and 2013, the number of strikes in Yemen was as high as or higher than in Pakistan. Although the availability of yearly strike data for Somalia is limited, there have certainly been fewer overall strikes and those that have taken place are episodic. Instead, the United States has relied more on proxies, such as African Union peacekeepers, with periodic strikes of its own against high-value targets from al-Shabab, a militant group affiliated with al-Qaeda in Somalia.[28]

The question that arises is why drone strikes have declined in Pakistan but increased in Yemen. One argument has to do with Pakistani diplomatic pressure limiting how often the United States resorts to drone strikes. In his address to the United Nations General Assembly, Pakistani Prime Minister Nawaz Sharif repeated calls he had made to end American drone strikes on the basis that they are a "violation of our territorial integrity . . . and must be waged within the framework of international law."[29] Although some accounts suggest that the Pakistani government tacitly supports the strikes, at least publicly the government has condemned them and the Pakistani public appears to be opposed, with the United States less popular now than during the Bush Administration, creating tensions in the bilateral relationship.[30] To the extent that there has been a diplomatic backlash, this factor does not appear to be especially convincing, as even Secretary of State Kerry's efforts to reassure Pakistanis angry about drone strikes conceded that the timeline would be set by the goals of the counterterrorism program: "I think the program will end as we have eliminated most of the threat and continue to eliminate it."[31]

Another, perhaps more plausible, explanation is analogous to the answer given by former bank robber Willie Sutton when asked why he robbed banks: "because that's where the money is." Indeed, the most straightforward and likely reason why drone strikes have decreased in Pakistan but increased in Yemen is that the United States has eliminated high-value targets in Pakistan, leaving few remaining targets. Meanwhile, terrorist activity increased in Yemen, with al-Qaeda in the Arabian Peninsula (AQAP) forming in 2009 as a merging of Saudi and Yemeni al-Qaeda branches. The fall of former President Saleh left something of a governance vacuum that created an opportunity for AQAP, increasing its operations, planning foiled attacks, and providing targets for American counterterrorism operations, many of which have been high-profile ones such as the American Anwar al-Awlaki.[32] AQAP has emerged as the terrorist "franchise that is most likely and most capable to launch an international attack" on the West, which explains its emergence as the country to which most drone strikes have migrated.[33]

The rate of civilian casualties
While drone strikes have killed a number of suspected militants in countries outside active combat zones – including Pakistan, Yemen, and Somalia – there have also been a number of errant strikes that have killed civilians, particularly in Pakistan. As Table 2.2 shows, the estimated civilian casualties span a considerable range, especially in Pakistan where verifying casualties has been complicated by the geography of the tribal region. Moreover, given the fluid nature of combatants in these regions, the designation of civilian and militant is itself somewhat problematic. The American government, however, suggests that the civilian casualty rate that was relatively high in Pakistan in the initial period of the strike history has declined. Corroborating this account, the New America

Country	Total Strikes	Civilians Killed	Children Killed	Total Killed
Pakistan	381	416–951	168–200	2,537–3,646
Yemen	59–69	24–71	6	287–423
Somalia	4–10	0–16	0	9–30

Table 2.2 Casualties as a result of drone strikes, 2002–2013

Source: Bureau of Investigative Journalism (as of December 2013)

Foundation reports that by 2013, civilian fatalities in Pakistan had dropped to just four of the 153 total, a rate of less than 3% compared to a rate of 12% just two years earlier. However, others quibble with these figures, suggesting that the claim of fewer civilian casualties hinges on contested notions of combatant status, with more fatalities among civilians than the official numbers have suggested.[34] We return to this question of civilian casualties in more detail when we discuss proportionality in chapter 4.

Targeting practices

While the United Kingdom and Israel have also used drones in combat, the most prodigious user has been the United States. Because of the numbers and of the fact that the United States is the most militarily powerful country, its practices are more likely to be considered a precedent for other countries that subsequently make decisions about drone strikes. As Goldsmith and Posner note, customary international law, which is law based on state practice as opposed to treaties, "seems to track the interests of powerful nations."[35] In this spirit, we examine American targeting decisions in the following sections, focusing on who is targeted and under what circumstances, with an eye toward establishing what other countries would regard as a precedent for their own decisions.

Based on information that has emerged about drone strikes,

the policy has gone through several stages of development. Between 2002 and 2007, the Bush Administration began using drones to target suspected terrorists in a policy sometimes referred to as "targeted killings." These strikes focused on significant, high-value members of al-Qaeda or the Taliban. In 2008, President Bush authorized what have become known as "signature strikes" against suspected al-Qaeda and Taliban fighters in Pakistan. Also known as "crowd killing" or "terrorist attack disruption strikes," signature strikes target suspected militants who "bear the characteristics of al-Qaeda or Taliban leaders on the run."[36] Targets are selected on the basis of behavioral patterns, that is, "signatures," of suspected terrorists. In other words, signature strikes mean that the CIA and JSOC "fire on targets based solely on their intelligence signatures – patterns of behavior that are detected through signals intercepts, human sources and aerial surveillance, and that indicate the presence of an important operative or a plot against US interests."[37] According to another anonymous official, at the peak of drone operations in Pakistan in 2009 and 2010 as many as half of all kills were classified as signature strikes.[38] According to some accounts, the administration "in effect, counts all military-age males in a strike zone as combatants." One anonymous US official stated that "You don't necessarily need to know the guy's name. You don't have to have a ten-sheet dossier on him. But you have to know the activities this person has been engaged in."[39]

The White House has defended its drone policy in part through fact sheets: "the United States will use lethal force only against a target that poses a continuing, imminent threat to US persons."[40] However, it is unclear whether this principle applies to signature strikes because the Obama Administration has not clarified whether or not "signature" behavior must pose a direct and imminent threat to US persons. The definition of "continuing, imminent threats" is not publicly known but does not merely include individuals who are causing (or capable of causing) direct harm to the United States. For example, US drones have reportedly employed "double-tap" strikes which target individuals who are retrieving victims from a previous strike.[41] Thus, there is a vast scope of available targets, ranging from groups of military-aged men to high-ranking leaders.

Furthermore, American citizens living abroad whom the US government determines to be significantly aiding al-Qaeda or the Taliban can also be targeted.[42] In February 2013, a Department of Justice White Paper was leaked and published by NBC that summarized the legal groundwork and justification given to a Congressional oversight committee for using lethal drone force against American citizens.[43] The US government stated that it will target American citizens if "the targeted individual poses an imminent threat of violent attack against the US"; the individual could not be captured; and the action is consistent with the relevant laws of conflict.

Mapped onto these policies dealing with drone strikes are inputs to the targeting decisions: the individuals to be targeted and how they are selected and vetted within the government. According to anonymous Defense officials interviewed by the Associated Press, the Obama Administration keeps a target list of about two dozen names. The so-called "kill lists" include individuals, each of whom has an in-depth dossier that is regularly reviewed and monitored by several intelligence and defense agencies. The list is the result of an interagency process that discusses the basis for targeting the individual, including his or her involvement with al-Qaeda and its affiliates and whether he or she was engaged in activities directed at the United States.

In about 2010, the Obama Administration developed the "disposition matrix," or what the *Washington Post* referred to as a "next-generation capture/kill list." The move was a response to challenges that the government had encountered in cases such as the al-Qaeda operative, Ahmed Abdulkadir Warsame, who was caught off the coast of Yemen and eventually brought to New York after being interrogated on a ship for two months. As one administration official allegedly put it, "Warsame was a classic case of 'What are we going to do with him?'" Disposition, then, refers to the management or disposal of the members on the target list. It includes more detailed information on the individual's biography, contacts, extradition requests, and contingencies, so that the government can adjust its plans for handling the individual if some unexpected event – such as a medical issue that would be cause for bringing a captured terrorist into the United States for treatment – arises.[44] As Miller notes, the matrix "is meant to map out contingencies, creating an operational menu that spells out each agency's role in case a suspect surfaces in an unexpected spot."[45]

Who runs the drone program?
As discussed, the Pentagon has generally presided over strikes in places such as Afghanistan, Iraq, and Libya and the CIA is responsible for strikes outside areas of active combat such as Pakistan, Yemen, and Somalia. In 2013, the US government reported that it would shift all CIA drone operations to the US military. All legal authority for drone warfare would be centralized to USC Title 10, removing the CIA's legal capability from USC Title 50. Lethal missions would now be considered "traditional military activities" under Title 10 and would potentially lose their discretion as covert operations. In principle, the military would seem to be the appropriate home for drone strikes, as it is typically seen as having more careful and transparent targeting practices than the CIA, where many of the attacks have originated. Not only is the military seen as more transparent, it also has a system of

accountability whereby individuals are bound by the Uniform Code of Military Conduct, compared to the absence of such institutional checks for the CIA. Typical military operations operate within Title 10 of the US code, which maintains clear, accountable rules for military operations. Using military force under Title 10 requires the consent of local governments, which would somewhat exonerate the United States of violating airspace.

The question arises, however, as to whether the move to the military is a distinction without a difference. Indeed, reports suggest that a condition of CIA strikes in Pakistan has been that the Pakistani government be able to approve targets, suggesting that the strikes may not be complete unilateral violations of Pakistani sovereignty.[46] Perhaps more relevant is the alternative to the CIA. Under the proposals, drone operations would move to the Joint Special Operations Command (JSOC) within the military, raising the question of whether there is any transparency or oversight difference between CIA- and JSOC-operated strikes. JSOC is highly secretive, perhaps more so than the CIA. Many of its highly classified missions, such as the bin Laden killing, operate under Title 50, the authority for covert operations, a provision authorized by executive order in the Bush Administration. Still other missions, according to government sources, happen outside Title 50 and are unacknowledged, which raises the question of whether transparency necessarily improves by virtue of shifting to JSOC.[47]

In addition, the CIA offers some practical advantages. According to some accounts, the intelligence is better than that of JSOC, which is a concern that Senator Dianne Feinstein alluded to when asked about moving operations from the CIA to JSOC:

> We've watched the intelligence aspect of the drone program: how they function. The quality of the intelligence. Watching the agency exercise patience and discretion. The military

> [armed drone] program has not done that nearly as well. That causes me concern. This is a discipline that is learned, that is carried out without infractions. . . . It's not a hasty decision that's made. And I would really have to be convinced that the military would carry it out that way.[48]

Another, perhaps less convincing, concern is that whereas the CIA has plausible deniability, JSOC operations would be viewed as being authorized by the government; as such, if an operation goes awry, the government will be seen as having more direct links with the operation, complicating diplomatic efforts.[49] Thus, while the proposal to move drone operations to JSOC is a gesture toward calls for greater transparency, the shift may actually not increase transparency but merely provide legitimate cover for business as usual. It may also prove to be less effective because of alleged intelligence limitations and also because of the perceived sense that JSOC would have institutional endorsement compared to the sense of autonomy that could in some senses delocalize the blame for operations gone astray.

(Lack of) transparency on drone strikes

Whether about the nature of the policy or the basis for targeting specific individuals, the American government has been relatively silent. Until 2012, the Obama Administration refused to acknowledge the covert drone program due to security concerns.[50] Most information concerning drones strikes had come from anonymous interviews by US government officials or from unauthorized leaks. However, beginning in 2012, the administration began to be more forthcoming with information about drone strikes.

As Scott Shane has noted, one possible reason for increased transparency in 2012 is that the Obama Administration had sought to clarify the government's policy on drones in case Obama lost the 2012 election, leaving an "amorphous program" to his successor. Another hypothesis is that the public disclosure arose in a period of transition and internal conflict, in which "the Defense Department and the CIA continue[d] to press for greater latitude to carry out strikes; Justice Department and State Department officials, and the president's counterterrorism adviser, John O. Brennan, have argued for restraint."[51]

Another plausible reason for the Obama Administration's increasing transparency is the growing number of questions that have surfaced about the drone program. As Tara McKelvey observed, in the early years of the drone campaign, the media "fell short in its coverage of the Obama Administration's drone program,"[52] only increasing the level and critical nature of the coverage during 2009 and intensifying it in the following three years. The increased media scrutiny has been joined by civil and human rights groups that have pressured the administration to increase its transparency on the drone program. Indeed, not everyone is enamored of the technology. The United Nations (UN) has been explicitly critical of the US drone program. UN officials have stated that the United States has infringed Pakistan's sovereignty because "as a matter of international law the US drone campaign in Pakistan is therefore being conducted without the consent of the elected representatives of the people, or the legitimate Government of the State. It involves the use of force on the territory of another State without its consent."[53] In late 2012, the UN declared that it would investigate the legality and procedures of drone strikes, specifically examining alleged civilian casualties.[54]

A number of nongovernmental organizations have also criticized drone policy. In April 2013, the American Civil Liberties Union, Amnesty International, the Center for Civilians in Conflict, the Center for Constitutional Rights, Human Rights First, the Human Rights Institute, Human Rights Watch, Open Society Foundations, and two Global

Justice centers at New York University Law School published a joint letter to President Obama outlining their stance on and concerns about drone strikes and targeted killings. The tone and message of the letter starkly opposes current practices. The memo states that "in particular, we call on the administration to: publicly disclose key targeted killing standards and criteria; ensure that US lethal force operations abroad comply with international law; enable meaningful congressional oversight and judicial review; and ensure effective investigations, tracking and response to civilian harm."[55] Ethicists have wondered about "the extent to which militaries should be allowed to prioritize the defense of their own soldiers against damage to a civilian population,"[56] a question that is at the heart of moral critiques of drones that we discuss later.

Many of the Obama Administration's efforts at disclosure are cast in terms of responding to calls from governmental organizations and nongovernmental organizations to be more transparent in terms of how its practices are compatible with moral and legal obligations, with the National Security Council spokesperson saying that "we will continue to disclose as much as we can."[57] The result was a public relations effort designed to increase the transparency of the drone program. In 2012, the Obama Administration began releasing some information on personality strikes, beginning with former White House counterterrorism advisor John Brennan giving a speech defending the drone program at the Woodrow Wilson Center in Washington DC, stating: "In full accordance with the law – and in order to prevent terrorist attacks on the United States and to save American lives – the United States government conducts targeted strikes against specific al-Qaeda terrorists, sometimes using remotely piloted aircraft, often referred to publicly as drones."[58]

Since then, many of these speeches from various members of the Obama Administration, including the president himself, have provided various details about the drone campaign, such as admissions of civilian casualties and assertions that drones are necessary for counterterrorism operations.[59] The aforementioned Department of Justice White Paper inadvertently increased transparency by a substantial margin when it was leaked to NBC in February 2013. Although Attorney General Eric Holder and other Obama Administration officials had outlined the basic legal conclusions, this paper was a much more detailed summary. Nonetheless, it only focused explicitly on targeting American citizens, a debate that the government itself has not resolved, judging from additional leaks about whether to target a specific American in Pakistan.[60]

In May 2013, the White House more formally sought to increase the sense of transparency of the drone policy. It published a fact sheet and President Obama gave a major speech on the drone program, which outlined the policy standards and procedures for the use of force in counterterrorism operations outside the United States. It emphasized a policy of capture over kill; of force only for "imminent threats"; and of the need for "near certainty that the terrorist target is present" and "near certainty that non-combatants will not be injured or killed." Reiterating the themes of the former legal advisor to the State Department Harold Koh's 2010 speech on the subject, the United States stood its ground in terms of how drones adhere to international law.[61]

Despite public discussion of "official rules" for drone strikes, there still remains a high level of ambiguity in determining which targets truly meet the various thresholds for lethal drone force. According to its defenders, the May 2013 public relations efforts offered transparency about targeting policies that had been increasingly demanded of the Obama Administration. As American University Law Professor Ken Anderson wrote, "the public presumably has greater confidence that there is a more morally and legally defensible policy in place, on the one hand, because a standard has been publicly stated and it is a high one."[62] As Goldsmith has written, however, the attempts at transparency "are conveyed in limited, abstract, and often awkward terms. They usually raise more questions than they answer."[63] For example, the administration has been vague in defining words such as "imminent" and unspecified conditions under which capturing an individual is more dangerous than killing him. In particular, the Obama Administration has not publicly spoken about signature strikes, provided a legal justification,[64] defined what qualifies as a "signature" that would warrant a drone strike, revealed how many people (and civilians) have been killed by signature and personality strikes, or responded to Congressional requests about signature strikes.[65] For example, in a letter to then CIA director nominee John Brennan, Senator John McCain asked, "How do 'signature strikes square with your statement that targeted killing operations are only approved when a targeted individual poses a 'significant threat to US interests?'"[66] It is unclear to what extent the CIA employs signature strikes, with some anonymous sources even claiming that most drone strikes are signature strikes, rather than targeted killings.[67] Senator McCain did not receive a response from Brennan, a result that is not uncommon regarding questions about signature strikes.

Drone proliferation

While the United States is the country that has used drones most frequently, a number of other countries have used them, have armed drones in their possession, or are in the process of acquiring some form of drone. The GAO has found that the number of countries with drones has increased dramatically in the last decade. In 2005, forty-one countries had some form of drone capability; by 2011, that number was seventy-six, although few of these countries currently have armed drones. This trend will not soon reverse: according to the Teal Group, global spending on UAV research, procurement, and development will surpass an estimated US$94 billion over the next decade.[68] As the GAO notes,

> The majority of foreign UAVs that countries have acquired fall[s] within the tactical category. Tactical UAVs primarily conduct intelligence, surveillance, and reconnaissance missions and typically have a limited operational range of at most 300 kilometres. However, some more advanced varieties are capable of performing intelligence collection, targeting, or attack missions. Mini UAVs were also frequently acquired across the globe during this period.[69]

Currently, the two main suppliers of drone technology are the United States and Israel. During the period between 2005 and 2011, the United States approved drone transfers to fifteen different countries, including Denmark, Italy, Lithuania, the United Kingdom, Australia, Colombia, Israel, and Singapore, although the only country to have received armed drones from the United States is the United Kingdom. Despite the proliferation of drones, the only countries known to have used armed drones in combat are the United States, the United Kingdom, and Israel. Data for countries other than the United States is even spottier, but evidence suggests that the United Kingdom has increasingly relied on drone strikes in Afghanistan, with just fourteen in 2008 but seventy-three in 2011, as shown in Figure 2.3. As of July 2013, the British military had launched 299 drone strikes in Afghanistan, which was roughly fifty fewer than the United States (officially unacknowledged) had launched in Pakistan at that time. Evidence for Israel suggests that drone strikes were used to kill militants in Sinai (August 2013), during the November 2012 Gaza conflict, and in the Gaza War of late 2008 and early 2009.[70]

Besides these countries that have used drones in combat

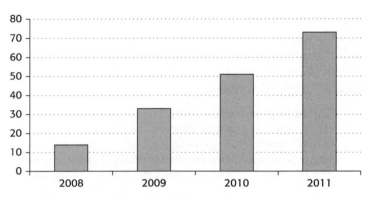

Source: Bureau of Investigative Journalism[71]

Figure 2.3 Number of drone strikes by the British military between 2008 and 2011 (Afghanistan)

are a number of others thought to already have combat drones or that are acquiring them. It appears that China and Iran also have armed drones, and France, Germany, India, Pakistan, Russia, Turkey, and the UAE are pursuing advanced armed drones.[72] Thus, although most of the seventy-six countries that the GAO lists are not seeking combat drones, most of the major international and regional powers have armed drones or are acquiring them. Countries with or pursuing armed drones are not only America's allies, such as Israel, Italy, and the United Kingdom, but also its competitors, such as China, Iran, and Russia.

On December 4, 2011, Iran reported that it had captured a largely intact RQ-170 sentinel drone, technology once exclusive to the United States' armed forces. An ultra-advanced UAV that has seen extensive use both in Afghanistan and Iran, the RQ-170 is most famous for providing the intelligence that led to the location of Osama bin Laden's compound. In the case of the captured drone, the CIA, which had been employing the drone to perform reconnaissance of Iran's nuclear facilities, lost contact with the RQ-170 early in its mission and reported it missing soon after. The CIA, which had been employing the drone to perform reconnaissance of Iran's nuclear facilities, lost contact with the RQ-170 early in its mission and reported it missing soon after. Though details are unclear regarding the nature of this failure – Iran claims to have targeted the drone in an "electronic attack" while the United States maintains that the drone simply malfunctioned – by December 8, Iran was broadcasting grainy footage showing what indeed appeared to be the missing RQ-170.[73] "The flights from Moscow and Beijing to Tehran were probably quite full the last few days,"[74] said P. W. Singer, a specialist in military robotics. Indeed, Russia and China did not hide their interest in inspecting the drone, most likely in the hope of pirating parts and reverse-engineering its technology.

Already, reports suggest that China has drones and considered using them in March 2013 to eliminate a drug trafficker in Myanmar who had allegedly targeted Chinese sailors. In playing out proliferation scenarios, the *National Journal* wondered "what happens if China arms one of its remote-piloted planes and strikes Philippine or Indian trawlers in the South China Sea? Or if India uses the aircraft to strike Lashkar-e-Taiba militants near Kashmir?" In September 2013, China sent a drone toward the contested Senkakus.[75] The UAV deployed was a surveillance drone, but nonetheless this had the effect of increasing tensions between China and Japan.

In short, while the United States has largely pioneered the use of drones, alongside the United Kingdom and Israel, the trend in drone use is toward rather than away from combat drones. The concluding chapter addresses the implications of drone proliferation, including the impact on regional stability and how leading states can help control proliferation, if not altogether, at least its adverse impacts.

Do drones work?

The last section of this chapter discusses the debate about whether drones "work." If drones are not effective, then it makes little sense to discuss the potential costs in terms of political, legal, and ethical legitimacy since the fundamental basis for their use would have no merit. The debate about effectiveness essentially divides into two camps. The first consists of those who believe drone strikes work by killing key leaders of the Taliban and al-Qaeda while also denying them sanctuary to plan attacks, thus saving American lives.[76] In contrast are those who believe that the strikes are creating more terrorists than they kill by aiding terrorist recruitment efforts, and that decapitation does not work because new leaders replace those who are killed.[77] While each side of the argument has its merits, we believe that the strategic ineffectiveness of drones outweighs their high tactical success rate.

The contours of each camp are fairly well established, but adjudicating between the two is more difficult, due to the classified nature of the drone campaign.[78] As mentioned earlier, the public does not officially know how many drone strikes the US government has carried out with what numbers of casualties; the best estimates put forth by various nongovernmental organizations (such as the New America Foundation and the Bureau of Investigative Journalism) are just that: estimates. In addition to the problem of data availability, there are methodological problems resulting from selection bias. Since the timing, location, and nature of targets are not randomly distributed, drawing inferences about the causal effect of strikes is difficult since the outcome may have been determined by factors independent of strikes; for example, the frequency of attacks may have been altered due to something such as a change of season.[79]

Patrick Johnston, who is in the pro-effectiveness camp,

addresses the methodological challenges by using failed decapitation attempts as controls for successful attempts – arguing that the failures are uncorrelated with the key variables – and employing a methodology called statistical matching to compare the organizational outcome that results from a strike that hits its target with one that does not. The difference between the two, he argues, is attributed to the causal impact of a strike. Using this approach, he finds that campaigns are more likely to end and insurgent attacks are less likely following the elimination of a terrorist leader, and that these strikes would likely increase government chances of a counter-insurgency victory.[80] Yet Johnston's approach is flawed because a successful strike is more likely to have resulted from targeting a group about which the United States had better intelligence or one that is less competent. If true, this would upset the balance of the matching approach. The success of the strike is not random. Nevertheless, Johnston's results are consistent with those of Bryan Price, who finds that drones increased the mortality rate of terrorist organizations, meaning that decapitated organizations were more likely to end than those that had not been subjected to leadership attacks.[81] The theoretical logic underpinning this finding is that organizations need leaders to function effectively and removing the leader affects whether the organization can recruit members.[82] Leaders are important, and eliminating those leaders undermines the effectiveness of the organization as a whole.

A somewhat less systematic argument in support of drone strikes refutes the opposition claim that drone strikes breed more terrorists than they eliminate. According to the American Security Project, while anti-American sentiment in drone-struck countries has definitively risen, "it is extremely difficult to single out drone strikes as a unique or even primary cause of anti-Americanism."[83] In Pakistan, people protest several US policies (such as the war in Afghanistan) and only particular drone strikes, rather than the entirety of them, tend to galvanize the population. Interestingly, in general urban Pakistanis have a hatred of drones, while Pakistanis in the tribal regions seem to give limited support to them, contending that they prefer drone strikes "over other alternatives like conventional military campaigns" or full-scale bombardments.[84] Again, polling in tribal regions in Pakistan, Yemen, and Somalia is often anecdotal and unverifiable. Certainly, drone strikes in these countries are perceived negatively overall; however, it is not a consistent, uniform hatred, as drones do seem to receive "guarded" support from tribal regions, but the inability to truly measure these sentiments hinders any in-depth analysis. That the strategic consequences are uncertain, but the tactical successes definitive, according to this camp merits continued drone strikes.

We find an alternative perspective more persuasive. It is not that leadership decapitation is entirely ineffective; drone strikes have certainly killed a number of suspected militants. As Obama suggested in his defense of the drone policy, strikes have killed twenty-two of the thirty top al-Qaeda leaders.[85] Others in his administration have suggested that drone strikes have "decimated" the al-Qaeda leadership.[86] While the strikes may have produced a number of tactical successes, we are skeptical that these translate into strategic effectiveness. As Audrey Kurth Cronin notes, even if targeted killings have decreased the number and lethality of strikes in Northwest Pakistan, they have little effect on "the group's ability to replace dead leaders with new ones. Nor have they undermined its propaganda efforts or recruitment."[87] A related point is that if the growing public opposition in places such as Yemen and Pakistan is any indication, the strikes have contributed to "visceral opposition."[88] The target of this opposition are the strikes themselves, triggering backlash among the populace; based in part on "martyrdom effects," decapitation intensifies the adversary's resolve in combat and in recruitment, making it easier to recruit new terrorists for the one that was killed.[89] Another target is the host government itself, which is delegitimized because another country has violated its airspace and territorial integrity, one of the most fundamental definitions of state legitimacy. The less legitimacy that a government commands, the less stability in that country and the more likely that country will be a breeding ground for additional terrorism. Most fundamentally, no counterterrorism strategy can be effective without addressing the economic and political reasons why individuals resort to terrorism in the first place.

Evidence for the argument that strikes are strategically ineffective compared to their relative tactical effectiveness comes in a number of forms. First, as Figure 2.4 shows, the differences between countries' support and opposition for drone strikes are considerable. Some of the largest differences are in Middle Eastern countries where presumably the United States would prefer to be viewed more favorably.[90] Although both the Pakistani and Yemeni governments have privately expressed support for the United States drone policy – with the Yemeni government being especially supportive and the recipient of considerable American aid – drone strikes are unpopular among the public.[91] In Yemen, drone strikes are "breeding anger and sympathy for al-Qaeda" from both tribal citizens in drone-targeted regions and political moderates in non-targeted Yemeni cities. Playing to their own domestic audiences, Pakistani political elites have channeled their public's concerns. Member of Parliament Imran Khan and Prime Minister Nawaz Sharif have both called for an end to drone strikes within Pakistan.[92]

To be sure, there is some evidence that, despite these top-line poll figures, support varies in important ways. As mentioned, while Pakistanis as a whole might not be enamored, those closer to the tribal areas appear *less* opposed. *The*

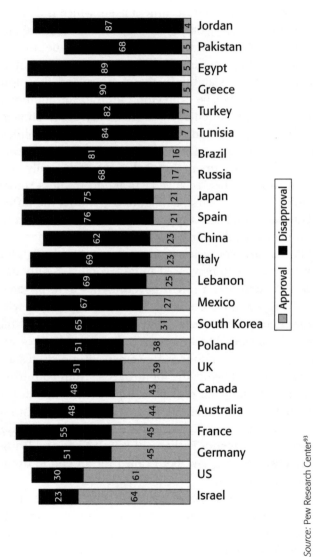

| | Approval | Disapproval |

Jordan 87 / 4
Pakistan 68 / 5
Egypt 89 / 5
Greece 90 / 5
Turkey 82 / 7
Tunisia 84 / 7
Brazil 81 / 16
Russia 68 / 17
Japan 75 / 21
Spain 76 / 21
China 62 / 23
Italy 69 / 23
Lebanon 69 / 25
Mexico 67 / 27
South Korea 65 / 31
Poland 51 / 38
UK 51 / 39
Canada 48 / 43
Australia 48 / 44
France 55 / 45
Germany 51 / 45
US 30 / 61
Israel 23 / 64

Source: Pew Research Center[93]

Figure 2.4 International approval and disapproval of US drone strikes, 2013

Economist conducted field interviews and found that people in these regions favored drone strikes over Pakistan's use of artillery, that the strikes were fairly accurate, and that they generally killed people who posed threats to the populace as well.[94] Nonetheless, just 5 percent of the overall population supports the policy, a meager foundation on which to base a legitimate sustainable policy.

A second form of evidence is the number of terrorists that occupy regions such as the Arabian Peninsula, home of AQAP, during the period of drone strikes. As Zenko observes, in 2010, the administration suggested that there were "several hundred al-Qaeda members" in the Arabian Peninsula. Two years later, after a number of drone strikes, there were "more than a thousand" and in 2012 AQAP had increased in number to "a few thousand."[95] Of course, the counterfactual question that arises is how many terrorists there would have been absent the drone strikes – perhaps thousands more – but the correlation is not encouraging: more drone strikes have corresponded with a large increase in terrorists.

A third way to argue the strategic ineffectiveness of drone strikes is to consider an organization's operations in the periods after strikes. Jenna Jordan's work has analyzed whether decapitation strikes are effective, which she operationalized as the group's decisiveness (whether it remained active) and organizational degradation after the strike. According to her analysis, the rate of collapse for decapitated groups is lower in general, suggesting that decapitation is "actually counterproductive," although "small, young, or ideological groups tend to be susceptible to leadership removal."[96] However, the groups that are susceptible are not those that are typically targeted by drones in the counterterrorism campaign; indeed, groups such as al-Qaeda are fairly resistant.

A fourth form of evidence dealing with the strategic ineffectiveness of drones are UN investigation claims that drone strikes have led to an increase in radicalized young men seeking revenge. Like many human rights groups, the UN reports that the drone strikes in the tribal regions were invoking local tribal law which "prescribed revenge for the loss of a life and that this entrenched tribal tradition had given rise to a desire, particularly among young men, to seek revenge for the drone strikes, thus radicalizing a new generation."[97] While this may be true in anecdotal circumstances, it is admittedly difficult to verify actual trends or disprove claims by the US officials that drone strikes are (on the whole) effective at disrupting the insurgency. In this UN report, even the Special Rapporteur admits that the findings were "largely anecdotal," but still "supported the conclusion that the strikes were frequently cited as a source of radicalization to violent extremism among younger Pashtun males."[98] Although a difficult methodological question, such qualitative evidence tracing the relationship between drone strikes and incentives for young men is persuasive.

The preceding analysis suggests that, from a tactical perspective, drones have succeeded in exactly the way the government has described: they have killed dozens of al-Qaeda militants and disrupted terrorist activities while minimizing the danger to American troops. Moreover, the threat of drone strikes has substantially degraded terrorist groups' capacity. Drones make it very difficult for terrorist organizations to communicate for fear that intercepted electronic communications will be used for establishing information about targets – a concern likely exacerbated by recent revelations about US National Security Agency penetration of terrorist communication networks. Drones also greatly increase the risk to large-scale terrorist training activities since congregating in open spaces leaves militants open to attack.

Nevertheless, from a strategic perspective, the effectiveness of drone strikes is less clear. By some accounts, they have contributed to rising anti-American sentiments in Pakistan, Yemen, and Somalia, and aided the recruitment of terrorists in these countries. As General McChrystal, former Commander of United States forces in Afghanistan, concluded, "the danger of special operating forces is that you get this sense that it is satisfying, it's clean, it's low risk, it's the cure for most ills." However, he added that the "too-heavy reliance on drones is also 'problematic' because 'it's not a strategy in itself; it's a short-term tactic.'"[99] Indeed, despite short-term success in preventing terrorist organization training and communication, drone strikes may actually cause splintering of groups into independent actors – thereby creating a more diffuse and insidious threat. From a political standpoint, as we will discuss in the next chapter, the incentives favor the fact that, in the short term, the effects are more clear-cut: the strikes kill important suspected terrorists, making it less likely that elected leaders will experience attacks on their watch. Politicians may think they can find ways to cope with the longer-term effects that may be less sanguine.

Although we believe that drone strikes ultimately create nearly as many problems as they solve, we would be remiss if we denied the significant utility of drones in very specific scenarios. First, drones may be effective when a decapitation strategy is best suited to a militant group's organizational dynamics – for example, when a leader is vital to that organization's ability to operate. Second, drones are occasionally a good option when police action or capture is impossible. In these cases, some scholars would argue that the imminence requirement does not hold. Finally, targeted killing may be the best choice given extremely high stakes, namely, if a terrorist organization were to acquire a nuclear device. This scenario would require swift action that might employ armed drones.

Conclusion

In a major speech about his administration's drone policy in May 2013, President Obama admitted that the United States had come to rely too heavily on drones because of their efficiency in eliminating terrorist leaders.[100] The increase in drone strikes, particularly during the Obama Administration, supports that statement, with the number of attacks growing steeply in its first term. Thus what began with related isolated strikes in the years immediately after 9/11 accelerated during the Obama Administration.

While the administration has argued that drone strikes are an effective part of its counterterrorism policy, there is a persuasive counterargument, which is that the strikes are tactically effective but strategically ineffective: they may kill particular terrorists in the short term but contribute to more terrorists in the long term. As the proliferation story suggests, other countries seem to have internalized the lesson that drone strikes work. The rate of proliferation and amount being spent on research and development and the number of key countries acquiring drones points to a growing market for drone technology and, most likely, the propensity for other countries to rely on drones in combat as the United States has. We return to the question of drone proliferation – in particular, how to control the spread of drones and especially the way they are used in combat – in the concluding chapter.

The next three substantive chapters, however, build on this "nuts and bolts" chapter. The first of these explores the politics of drones and why the democratic system of checks and balances has largely punted on the drone policy. From there, it turns to the question of whether drone strikes are compatible with international law, a criticism alluded to in this chapter. We then turn to the morality of drone strikes in the final substantive chapter before the conclusion.

CHAPTER THREE

Drones and Democracy

Introduction

In his 2009 Nobel Peace prize acceptance speech, President Barack Obama observed that "war, in one form or another, appeared with the first man . . . we must begin by acknowledging the hard truth that we will not eradicate violent conflict in our lifetimes." Obama's message was not purely realist, however; he went on to credit post-World War II international norms and multilateral security institutions with reducing the cost of recent wars. Yet the president failed to mention a critical factor underlying the changing nature and conduct of conflict: domestic politics. In democracies, the populace bears the burden of war, creating a strong incentive to depress the costs of conflicts. Democratic leaders, who are held to account by voters, must consider this incentive when creating foreign policy.

Drones introduce greater moral and political complexity into this calculus by decreasing and rendering less visible the costs of war. The desire to minimize expenditures of wartime blood and funds explains the allure of airpower in general, as well as the growing reliance on drones in particular. While the shift to drones appears to lower costs – by substituting unmanned for manned aircraft – there are unintended consequences that must be considered. Without apparent costs, what mechanisms hold leaders accountable? By not bearing the burden, does the populace give tacit approval to perpetual war? Does the American public perceive an expansive enough self-interest to insist on accountability for targeted killings prosecuted overseas, or will wars that affect other populaces continue unnoticed in the background? Is the result a global battlefield, with wars limited by neither time nor space? Does the US political system have the capacity for rigorous oversight of drone policy?

This chapter grounds these questions in the democratic accountability literature, which suggests that the democratic conduct of war is likely to be influenced by populaces that bear the burden of, and thus put the brakes on, costly conflicts. Having spelled out the theoretical expectations associated with democratic peace, we then outline the effects of democratic accountability on the ways that democracies fight wars, focusing on drones as a vehicle for minimizing the domestic costs of conflict. Next, we discuss the unintended consequences of these efforts to minimize costs, presenting evidence that the public's preferences reinforce the use of drones and that, in using drones, the public becomes increasingly detached from conflict. We then discuss the prospect for democratic checks coming from the legislative and judicial branches of government. Lastly, we identify the implications for democratic accountability and the prospects for peace.

The democratic dynamics of war[1]
In 1795, Immanuel Kant observed that cultural and technological forces would make military conflict more costly. This created the impetus for rational actors to avoid war's devastating effects by pursuing peace. He argued that all citizens – regardless of the type of polity – seek to protect themselves and their property, and those who live in liberal democracies have the unique power to shape state activities so as to achieve these objectives. Kant's "Perpetual Peace" responded to a political climate of eighteenth-century Europe

which was defined by the ambitions – both military and economic – of the aristocracy. In this essay, he articulated the relationship between oligarchy and military adventurism, contrasting it with the more precautionary force that democratic constituents placed on their leaders. He writes:

> In a constitution which is not republican, and under which the subjects are not citizens, a declaration of war is the easiest thing in the world to decide upon, because war does not require of the ruler, who is the proprietor and not a member of the state, the least sacrifice of the pleasures of his table, the chase, his country houses, his court functions, and the like.[2]

Kant, however, is quite clear that this situation does not apply to polities that are responsive to citizen preferences: "If the consent of the citizens is required in order to decide that war should be declared (and in this constitution it cannot but be the case), nothing is more natural than that they would be very cautious in commencing such a poor game, decreeing for themselves all the calamities of war."[3] In the centuries that followed Kant's initial observation, scholars applied democratic peace theory to a wide range of political and military situations, outlining the way that when a democratic citizenry pays the costs of war, it is generally judicious in selecting the wars it supports. Valentino et al. note that "The fact that elected leaders are more accountable to the citizens who must bear the costs of war does not imply that these leaders will avoid wars in general – only that they will oppose highly unpopular wars that threaten their tenure in office."[4] Along these lines, Reiter and Stam maintain that, because "the people ultimately pay the price of war in higher taxes and bloodshed," their political willingness to engage in conflict is conditional on its cost and necessity.[5] Kant's premises have found support in contemporary social science: that the public pays the costs of war; that shouldering these costs is usually highly unpopular; that under these circumstances, the public is only willing to participate in war efforts that warrant the costs that they incur; finally, that the citizenry has the electoral power to register its displeasure by ousting policy makers who are unable to honor their preferences.

Obviously, Kant was right when he predicted that the costs of modern conflict would grow exponentially in the nineteenth and twentieth centuries. He was also prescient to the extent that these costs would provide some impetus for nontrivial peace movements. Over the last fifty years, policy makers have witnessed the galvanizing of peace activists across the world on nuclear proliferation and the slogging "progress" of the Vietnam War.[6] For example, on April 18, 1960, between 60,000 and 100,000 UK citizens marched in London to protest the testing of hydrogen bombs.[7] Similar protest movements took this sort of demonstration as both instruction and inspiration. This widespread mobilization stands in marked contrast to the extremely limited and largely marginal peace protests in previous decades.[8] As discussed in the introduction, the justification for these protests against nuclear proliferation was shocking in its simplicity – these weapons stood to destroy modern civilization. As we have argued elsewhere, "Kant predicted that in representative democracies such as the United States, war protests would have the ability to revise policy and dramatically alter the course of military conflicts by demanding that governments be responsive to citizen interests and fears."[9]

Despite his prescience, Kant overlooked an important idea, an idea that often eludes contemporary social scientists as well. We suggest here that the motivating force to shield one's person and property will lead democratic publics to lobby for policies that protect them from the traditional costs associated with war, but these preventative measures are not in any way tantamount to peace. Drone warfare is an instructive case study. The differential between property protection and pacifism reintroduces the possibility of oligarchic decision-making. For example, citizens might urge lawmakers to take on more federal debt or adopt military technologies that shield forces from harm in order to avoid shouldering the direct costs of war, belying Kant's hope that precisely these costs would keep democracies out of aggressive conflict. Obviating popularly borne costs empowers democratic leaders to conduct affairs of state without public deliberation or support. In Paul Kahn's words, drone warfare "may take the destructive power of war outside of the boundaries of democratic legitimacy, because we are far more willing to delegate the power to use force without risk to the president than we are a power to commit the nation to the sacrifice of its citizens."[10] Kant gestured toward this danger in the preliminary articles to "Perpetual Peace" when he stated that no nation should incur debt in order to accomplish military objectives, suggesting that a nation's willingness to take on debt for military expenditures would be directly proportional to its willingness to go to war. This has, of course, become general practice for many modern polities and has caused a great deal of tension in the international community – just as Kant predicted.[11] Kant, however, did not predict unmanned technologies.

US foreign policy in the second half of the twentieth century reflected the correlation between debt and militarism that Kant underscored. Especially after the Vietnam War, leaders attempted to shield their citizens from war-depleted treasure. For example, since 1968, American leaders have managed to sidestep an historical mainstay of US war finance, war tax. Of course this meant that debt incurred for military expenditures spiked dramatically. While the US citizenry has no love for debt, the relationship between debt and war is far more diffuse for most Americans than the rather immediate tie between war and a war tax.[12] This fact should come home to a reader in light of a *Washington Post* comment regarding war tax:

> The bill will bring daily, almost hourly, reminders to the
> people of the United States of the burden that is entailed in
> the prosecutions of a just and victorious war. The average
> citizen feels the effect of the war tax when he arises in the
> morning . . . he is reminded of it the last thing at night when
> he puts on his tax-assessed pajamas.[13]

Such unpopular bills restated the costs of military conflict,
causing individuals to reevaluate their support for military
action. The recent wars in Afghanistan and Iraq, in contrast,
have been just one source of debt among many (this source of
debt is rarely disambiguated from other sources). This makes
it considerably harder to isolate the wars' responsibility for
the financial crises of the past decade. We have argued elsewhere that, "While debt-driven war financing is not unique to
democracies, it is more likely in representative governments
because it attenuates short-term financial pressure on citizens
and, by extension, their elected representatives."[14]

In line with this discussion of the economic costs of war,
drone use aligns with new attitudes favoring war at minimal
cost. In the words of the Congressional Research service,
drones are "the poor man's air force."[15] As outlined in the
second chapter of this volume, the unit costs associated
with drones, compared with modern manned aircraft, tend
to be lower. Similarly, maintenance tends to be more cost-
effective.[16] However, as the systems have required more
sophisticated sensors, costs of UAVs have begun to move
toward parity with manned aircraft, making the economic
case for drones far from obvious. For example, in recent
years a debate has emerged about whether to retire the U-2
reconnaissance aircraft, replacing it with the Global Hawk
UAV. The Pentagon opted to delay the retirement of the
U-2 after a careful cost-benefit analysis. Deputy Secretary of
Defense Ashton Carter observed that the Global Hawk had
"priced itself out of the niche in terms of taking pictures in

the air ... that's a disappointment for us, but that's the fate of things that become too expensive in a resource-constrained environment."[17] On the whole, however, drones continue to be a cost-effective alternative to modern manned systems. As the British land forces Chief of the General Staff General Sir David Richards concluded, "one can buy a lot of UAVs or Tucano aircraft for the cost of a few Joint Strike Fighters and heavy battle tanks."[18]

The effort to spare citizens from direct exposure to the loss of treasure in war matches democracies' efforts to spare them the loss of blood. In addition to moving to an all-volunteer force after Vietnam, the United States increasingly relies on technologies that reduce the risk to its own soldiers and even make troop involvement obsolete. Drones represent the culmination of this trend. As Peter Singer noted, there is currently not a single aerospace manufacturer that is dedicating its energies toward the development of new manned aircraft.[19] If we look at the rhetoric surrounding the development of combat drones, much of it turns on troop protection and the ability to project force without risk. As the Congressional Research Service suggested, "UAVs offer two main advantages over manned aircraft: they are considered more cost-effective, and they minimize the risk to a pilot's life."[20] In the words of Phillip Everts, "total reliance is put today in the effectiveness of military technology, 'smart weapons' and 'airpower.' The prospect of a war without bloodshed – at least on one's own side – is cherished."[21]

The calculation in terms of force protection is definitive and will most likely outweigh the considerations of drones' economic advantages. This was a factor (in addition to the pressure of corporate lobbies) in Congress's support for the Global Hawk acquisition and development, regardless of the aircraft's lack of support in the United States Air Force (USAF). Governments using drones have been clear about their antipathy toward troop losses. British Defence Minister Philip Dunne suggested a greater reliance on UAV technologies when he applauded them for "saving the lives of British and ISAF [International Security Assistance Force] personnel in Afghanistan."[22] When violence increased dramatically in 2009, President Obama was confronted with a political double-bind: how could he maintain US forces in Afghanistan while also upholding the tacit promise to the American people that they would no longer have to shoulder the burden of warfare. The answer was apparently simple: in his first term, he authorized over six times more drone strikes than George W. Bush.[23]

The domestic politics of drone usage

As the previous section suggests, the turn to drone strikes, especially in the context of rising coalition fatalities, is not surprising because it reduces the risk for US military personnel and eliminates the risk to pilots. Evidence suggests this is good domestic politics. As we show in the following sections, although the US public may have some qualms about drone strikes, it is generally unopposed to the policy. Moreover, the executive branch oversees the drone war, and the legislative and judicial branches have largely stepped aside rather than introduce roadblocks into the policy. Taken together, the checks and balances theoretically associated with democratic institutions have been inoperative, as the public and the legislative and judicial branches of government have generally remained silent about, or expressed support for, the drone program. The result is that the executive has enjoyed considerable latitude in shaping drone policy, allowing the policy to continue relatively unfettered and unexamined. In the conclusion to this chapter, we consider the implications of such freedom of action, namely the possibility of conflict that is boundless in time and space.

The American public and the use of drones

While Americans (65 percent) report that they have heard something or a lot about the use of drones, a sizable minority (about 35 percent) indicates that they have heard just a little or nothing about their use.[24] However, hearing something about drones does not appear to translate into understanding how they are used. For example, in 2012 a plurality of Americans either did not know where drone strikes were used most or responded with the wrong country.[25] Despite the confusion over how and when drones are employed, the American public is generally supportive of their use, as a compilation of polls on drone use shows in Table 3.1.

The public's enthusiasm for drones has become part of the political narrative, amplified by media outlets trumpeting "The American Public Loves Drones," as one *Washington Post* headline proclaimed.[26] Whether the public actually has qualms about the policy is rarely broached in survey questions. There are no polls that raise the question of legal authorization, for example.[27] Thus, to the extent that they propagate the government's position on drone policy – for example, describing targets as suspected terrorists despite their sometimes-contested status – polls contribute to the prevailing narrative about the public's support for drones. A typical formulation is the following from a Yougov/ *Economist* poll: "Do you approve or disapprove of the Obama Administration using drones to kill high-level terrorism suspects overseas?" Or another (Gallup): "Do you think the US government should or should not use drones to . . . launch airstrikes in other countries against suspected terrorists?" And the NBC/*Wall Street Journal* version: "Do you favor or oppose the use of unmanned aircraft, also known as drones, to kill suspected members of Al Qaeda and other terrorists?" As we suggest in chapter 4 on international law, however, the language of these polls takes as a given what is often the

Table 3.1 Public opinion data on support for drone strikes (polls taken between 2011 and 2013)

Date	Source	Support (%)	Oppose (%)	Don't Know (%)
2013				
July	Pew Research	61	30	8
June	NBC/*WSJ*†	66	16	15
June	CBS/*NYT*	72	22	6
April	CBS/*NYT*	70	20	10
March	Gallup	65	28	8
March	Fox News	74	22	4
March	*Economist*/YouGov	80	11	9
February	NBC/WSJ	64	12	22
February	*Economist*/YouGov	49	19	32
February	*Economist*/YouGov	48	19	33
February	*Economist*/YouGov	51	19	30
February	Fairleigh Dickinson	75	13	12
February	Fairleigh Dickinson	65	21	13
2012				
June	Pew Research	62	28	10
February	ABC/*WashPost*	83	11	6
2011				
October	Pew Research†	86	8	2
September	Pew Research	68	19	13
July	Pew Research	86	8	5

Note: Some of the totals do not add up to 100% because of rounding
† Poll had a residual "depends" answer category, which is excluded from the results presented

Table 3.2 Concern with the possibility that drones are harming innocent civilians				
Date	Source	Concerned	Not Concerned	Don't Know
June 2013	CBS/*NYT*	84%	13%	2%
February 2013	Pew Research	81%	15%	4%
June 2012	Pew Research	94%	4%	2%

contested status of the target. By appearing to have settled the issue of combatant status and legal authorization, polls constrain the ideological space of the drone debate and contribute to the prevailing view that drone strikes enjoy high levels of support among the domestic public.

A few polls do query individuals about combatant status and hint at individuals' concern with whether drones are harming innocent civilians (see Table 3.2). These questions, however, are stand-alone, making it difficult to isolate the effect of combatant status on public support since there is no randomized baseline against which to compare the treatments. Moreover, they only gauge concern with harming civilians when perhaps a more important question is whether individuals support drone strikes conditional on those strikes harming civilians.

To the extent that polls have exhibited variation in individual responses depending on victim status, the questions deal with the question of targeting US citizens or individuals on US territory. The responses printed in Table 3.3 suggest that the public is quite negative when hypothetical drone strikes hit too close to home, with support dropping the more US-focused the target becomes. Support for strikes against an American in the United States registered just 13% in a March 2013 Gallup survey. Similarly, a February 2012 poll found that only 9% of Americans registered their opposition to a policy of using drones for targeted killing in general, compared to 52% who indicated that they oppose using drones

Table 3.3 Support for drone strikes given different citizen and territory status			
Target Status	Support	Oppose	Don't Know
Suspected terrorists	65%	28%	8%
US citizens living abroad	41%	52%	7%
In the USA against terrorists	25%	66%	9%
In the USA against US citizens who are suspected terrorists	13%	79%	7%
Source: Gallup, March 25, 2013			

for domestic, unarmed surveillance.[28] This finding is striking because the distinction suggests greater concern with civil liberties at home than the legal and ethical implications of using drones abroad – such as sovereignty violations (as in Pakistan, Yemen, and Somalia, where the United States has used drones), the question of killing American citizens abroad without due process, and the international legal principles of distinction and proportionality related to killing civilians.

As the evidence above suggests, the apparent popularity of drones gives leaders incentives to rely on drones for counterterrorism. Added to these political incentives is the political toxicity of detaining suspected terrorists. The Bush Administration received considerable criticism for its detention policies, especially Guantanamo Bay, yet the Obama Administration felt domestic pressure to continue the aggressive counterterrorism policies of the Bush Administration. As Ken Anderson observed, "since the US political and legal situation has made aggressive interrogation a questionable activity anyway, there is less reason to seek to capture rather than kill. . . and if one intends to kill, the incentive is to do so from a standoff position because it removes potentially messy questions of surrender."[29] While the government has denied this connection between the unpopularity of Guantanamo and the decision to kill rather than capture – Attorney General Eric Holder reported that the increase in targeted killing "is not a function of not trying to take people to Guantanamo" – the intuition behind the connection remains sound.

As Mark Mazzetti has argued, the lack of clear, politically palatable detention policies creates political incentives to avoid capturing suspected terrorists. Drawing on numerous interviews, he notes: "Killing was the preferred course of action in Somalia, and as one person involved in the mission planning put it, 'We didn't capture him because it would have been hard to find a place to put him.'"[30] He also quoted former CIA lawyer John Rizzo acknowledging that Obama officials "never came out and said they would start killing people because they couldn't interrogate them, but the implication was unmistakable . . . Once the interrogation was gone, all that was left was the killing."[31] Drones would seem to offer a more politically benign alternative, one that would circumvent uncomfortable questions about how to interrogate, where to detain, and in what capacity to try the suspected terrorists. As Mazzetti concluded, the politics favored drones over detention because "interrogation and detention were so controversial, and because no prominent Democrat had opposed drone strikes and Republicans wouldn't oppose Obama 'for fighting *too* aggressive a campaign against terrorists.'"[32] In short, the data and logic suggest that the use of drones is good politics – at least, good domestic politics. The use of drones provides a win–win proposition for the president, who could appear strong on defense without responsibility for body bags coming home, a development that would likely send his political fortunes tumbling.

The evolution of American drone policy demonstrates how financial and technological engineering has exposed a loophole in Kant's democratic peace theory. By distancing citizens from the personal and financial risks of war, modern

warfare – and drone warfare in particular – gives individuals little incentive to challenge their leaders' conduct of war.
How the United States conducts its wars – whether wartime
considerations of civilian casualties (which we will discuss
in the next chapter), or lethal action in countries with which
the United States is technically not at war (such as Yemen,
Somalia, and Pakistan) – receives little scrutiny.

Democratic checks and balances?

According to democratic logics of accountability, the public is
just one potential check on leaders' conduct of wars abroad;
the legislative and judicial branches should also play important roles. For separate reasons, however, neither branch has
exercised meaningful oversight of drone policy. The executive
branch exclusively drafts and vets the infamous "kill list" with
little or no input from other branches of government.[33] The
following sections explain the potential legislative and judicial
checks on drone policy and assess the plausibility of either
branch playing a more active policy role. Ultimately, the executive has had enormous latitude in conducting war, a feature
of the strong American presidency, which favors considerable
executive autonomy in key foreign policy decisions such as
the use of drones.

The legislative branch
By keeping US troops out of harm's way, drones not only mute
public resistance, they also shield their use from legislative
checks. When asked why drone strikes in Yemen and Libya
did not require Congressional – and therefore, indirectly,
public – oversight, the Obama Administration answered that
the strikes did not endanger US troops.[34] According to the
Administration's interpretation of the War Powers Resolution,
drones are not covered because the Resolution only requires

that the President obtain Congressional approval when deploying troops for more than sixty days. A more frequently cited domestic legal justification for drone strikes is the Authorization for Use of Military Force (AUMF). After 9/11, the United States Congress authorized the use of military force, allowing the president to target those who "planned, authorized, committed, or aided the terrorist attacks" of 9/11. As then counterterrorism advisor John Brennan argued, "these targeted strikes are legal . . . as a matter of domestic law . . . there is nothing in the AUMF that restricts the use of military force against al-Qaeda to Afghanistan."[35]

If either rationale is correct, the Administration is justified in suggesting that it does not need Congressional approval for its drone policy or for specific strikes. However, there are reasons to be dubious about this claim. First, the threshold for the War Powers Resolution is not whether troops are in harm's way but rather whether they are "introduced into hostilities or into situations where imminent involvement in hostilities is clearly indicated by the circumstances."[36] Drone strikes obviously cross that threshold. Another question deals with whether the AUMF covers strikes in places such as Somalia and Yemen. According to Bruce Ackerman, the move to target "suspicious behavior" by groups such as al-Qaeda in the Arabian Peninsula (AQAP), which operates in Somalia and Yemen, would require additional Congressional authorization.[37] Worried about a "boundless global war on terror," President Obama has questioned the viability of the AUMF more than a decade after its passage, but members of Congress themselves have defended it out of concern that its modification would lead to a slackening of assertive counter-terrorism policies.[38]

Indeed, despite contested domestic legal authorization for the Obama Administration's drone policy, Congress has essentially abdicated oversight responsibility. As Zenko suggested in a Council on Foreign Relations report, "despite nearly ten years of nonbattlefield targeted killings, no congressional committee has conducted a hearing on any aspect of them."[39] Congress is privy to some details of the program through the House and Senate Intelligence Committees but broader scrutiny is limited because of the covert nature of the program and members of Congress have not demanded it. For bureaucratic theories of politics, such nonchalance might seem puzzling since we might expect an instinct for aggrandizement and checking if at all possible the relatively unconstrained executive powers on when and how drones are used abroad.[40]

As Kenneth Schultz has observed, however, Congress has incentives to be risk averse on foreign policy. It gets little credit when things go well since counterterrorism success is rarely captured in a news story; success is a non-event, such as a terrorist attack that never comes to fruition or a soldier who does not die. Congress gets considerable blame, however, if it votes against stronger security measures and things go badly, as when a terrorist attack does occur; or votes for an intervention and a soldier dies in combat. Congress's strongest incentive is to wash its hands of oversight responsibility, deferring to the executive's prerogatives over drone policy.[41] As Amy Zegart argued about Congressional oversight of national security more generally, "legislators have weak incentives and blunt tools," resulting in "only sporadic and ineffectual oversight" of the national security bureaucracy.[42]

To the extent that members of Congress have pushed for greater oversight, they are motivated more by the concerns about the rights of American citizens, whether in terms of targeting or surveillance. In March 2013, Republican Senator Rand Paul held a thirteen-hour filibuster to block the confirmation of CIA Director John Brennan, but the content and coverage of his stand focused almost exclusively on unchecked power with respect to Americans. As the *New York Times* summarized it: "The debate goes to the heart of a deeply rooted American suspicion about the government, the military and the surveillance state: the specter of drones streaking through the skies above American cities and towns, controlled by faceless bureaucrats and equipped to spy or kill."[43]

Legislators and the media tend to focus their critiques largely on the surveillance and targeting of American citizens, which have constituted a fraction of the drone activities to date. For example, in a *New Yorker* critique of the Obama Administration's drone program, Jane Mayer points to an op-ed by Georgetown Law professor David Cole that "raised what is perhaps the gravest concern: the president's assertion of a secret, unchecked power to kill even Americans with no due process or public accountability."[44] However, the four Americans killed in drone strikes – Anwar al-Awlaki, specifically targeted by the United States, and three others not specifically targeted but killed: Samir Khan, Abdulrahman Anwar al-Awlaki (al-Awlaki's son), and Jude Mohammed[45] – represent just four of about 5,000 individuals in Pakistan, Yemen, and Somalia killed in the drone program. To be sure, the concern is with the direction in which unchecked power could take the government, or, as Cole writes, "how can we be free if our government has the power to kill us in secret?" But the implications for war and peace more broadly turn on international casualties and the scope of the drone program. To rephrase Cole's question: how can there be peace if our government has the power to kill others in secret?

In short, the legislature's electoral incentives are oriented around the protection of its own citizens' interests, which are local rather than global. It has therefore not served a meaningful restraining or oversight function in terms of the drone program, choosing a more risk-averse approach of deferring to the executive rather than trying to check its powers. As the next section will suggest, while some individuals within the judicial branch have sought to limit the unfettered executive power on drones, the institution as a whole has not.

Judicial checks and balances
The confirmation hearings for CIA Director John Brennan presented one of the rare moments where political elites, even if temporarily, called for greater oversight of the drone policy. Senator Angus King (Independent Senator from Maine) expressed concern with the concentration of power in the Obama Administration's counterterrorism policy, particularly the use of drones and targeted killings. He cautioned that "having the executive being the prosecutor, the judge, the jury, and the executioner all in one is very contrary to the traditions and laws of this country."[46] But even as King and his Congressional colleagues belatedly sought to limit executive privilege over drone policy, he advocated increased oversight by the judicial – not the legislative – branch.

To date, the courts have had little influence on the drone policy other than as a permissive element, though some individuals have tried to exercise principled restraints. In a case brought by the relatives of three Americans killed in Yemeni drone strikes – Anwar al-Awlaki, Samir Khan, and Abdulrahman – Judge Rosemary Collyer indicated that she was "troubled" by the notion that the executive could kill Americans without any role for the courts or any form of due process. The executive had made the case that courts do not have the expertise to adjudicate the threat posed by individual terrorists and that the executive branch has its own form of "checks" on executive decision-making. During oral arguments, Judge Collyer responded, sardonically, "The executive is not an effective check on the executive."[47]

This case echoes some of the broader concerns about judicial checks on the executive's hand in drone policies.

Generally, proposals for greater judicial oversight call for special courts, adjudicating legality pre-strike or post-strike. Post-strike drone courts would be relatively simple: if an unjust drone strike occurred against an individual, the target (or their family) could take a suit to the suggested court for compensation. This approach would have the court review what was known about the target, rather than question the judgment of the commander-in-chief before a strike.[48] It would not stop a strike but decisions that impugn a particular strike would cast a pall on the program and perhaps reduce the president's legitimacy. That said, if cases that challenge the constitutionality of previous strikes such as *al-Awlaki v. Panetta* are any guide, these proceedings may not be effective. In such cases, the government has a decisive upper hand, with special national security prerogatives that are likely to trump the plaintiff's case. The *Rasul v. Myers* outcome – in which the DC Circuit Court ruled that former Guantanamo prisoners who claimed they were tortured were not able to sue military personnel such as the Secretary of Defense – pointed in a footnote to "the danger of obstructing US national security policy."[49] Similarly, in a case about the legal justification for targeting American citizens, Judge Colleen McMahon ultimately ruled in favor of the government but declared, "I can find no way around the thicket of laws and precedents that effectively allow the executive branch of our government to proclaim as perfectly lawful certain actions that seem on their face incompatible with our Constitution and laws while keeping the reasons for their conclusion a secret."[50] As these cases suggest, the legal playing field is far from even.

The likely vehicle for legal oversight would be a pre-strike court charged with evaluating the legality of individual targeted killings before they are conducted. Pre-strike courts would most likely be modeled after the Foreign Intelligence Surveillance Act (FISA) courts, which are special, top-secret courts authorized by the 1978 legislation that addressed concerns about government spying in the wake of Watergate. The FISA court is, at its core, an extension of domestic law enforcement. It secretly issues search warrants without jeopardizing surveillance by reviewing and approving intelligence collection activities. The drone version would weigh in on the relative imminence of threat, whether the individuals could be captured instead, and whether the action is compatible with the laws of war. The court process would be initiated by the administration, which would file an application with the Counterterrorism (CT) Court by listing the individual and identifying probable cause behind the individual's connection with terrorism.[51]

Senators Dianne Feinstein (chairwoman of the Senate Intelligence Committee) (Democrat, California), Pat Leahy (chairman of the Senate Judiciary committee) (Democrat, Vermont), Chuck Grassley (Republican, Iowa), and Angus King (Independent, Maine) have expressed interest, or at least an interest in considering, the establishment of a drone court.[52] The most outspoken advocate for a drone court has been Senator King, who has publicly asked members of the Senate Intelligence Committee to "contemplate legislative solutions, such as the creation of an outside judicial process similar to the FISA court."[53] However, Senator King appears to favor drone courts that assess lethal strikes against US citizens, rather than the entirety of strike operations. At most, while there seems to be support from some Obama Administration officials, advocacy is mostly anonymous and unorganized.

Although the idea of judicial review seems appealing because it introduces checks and balances on a relatively unmonitored drone program, the prospect of courts presents practical difficulties. First, if a threat is actually imminent, the executive would still have unfettered authority to strike under international law, where the conception of imminence would be based on anticipatory self-defense and no special authorization would be necessary or possible. As legal scholar Neal Katyal noted, "it is hard to think of something less suitable for a federal judge to rule on than the fast moving and protean nature of targeting decisions."[54] Second, as Katyal also observed, "there is no true precedent for interposing courts into military decisions about who, what, and when to strike militarily."[55] A third issue deals with expertise and whether judges are in a position to adjudicate the wisdom of targeting decisions in the short timeframe in which they must render judgments.[56] In a lawsuit that sought to remove al-Awlaki from the targeted strike list, *Nasser al-Awlaki v. Barack Obama*, the United States District Court echoed a previous decision, *Reno v. Am.-Arab Anti-Discrimination Comm* (1999), which stated that courts tend to be "institutionally ill-equipped to assess the nature of battlefield decisions."[57]

Benjamin Powell, former general counsel for the Director of National Intelligence, said that "a number of thorny legal issues . . . with very complex implications" must be resolved before a FISA-style court is established.[58] These issues include specifying what the court would rule on, whether or not the court rulings would cover US citizens, and how these courts would interact with the president's constitutional power to defend the nation.[59] The executive branch has been skeptical of these proposals. In his May 23, 2013 speech on drone policy, President Obama remarked:

> I've asked my administration to review proposals to extend oversight of lethal actions outside of warzones that go beyond our reporting to Congress. Each option has virtues in theory, but poses difficulties in practice. For example, the establishment of a special court to evaluate and authorize lethal action has the benefit of bringing a third branch of government into the process, but raises serious constitutional issues about presidential and judicial authority.[60]

A separate issue with drone courts has less to do with whether the courts would impose too many unprecedented constraints than with whether they would simply be a "rubber stamp" for the executive branch's targeting decisions. Indeed, the tendency for the current FISA court to rubber stamp the US government's surveillance warrants, especially since the Court only hears the government's case, clouds assessments of a drone court's viability. If the FISA court approves almost all applications to gather private intelligence, would a drone court follow in a similar fashion? If so, what purpose would a drone court actually serve?

Perhaps more worrisome is evidence that FISA courts have expanded the "special needs" doctrine, which allows the government to undertake broader surveillance without specific warrants in order to "combat an overriding public danger." With broader authorization, the government has been able to access without a warrant far more information than was available prior to a 2008 change to the law.[61] Thus, while established to check the power of an overreaching executive during Vietnam and the Nixon years, the FISA court has actually loosened the reins, undermining the constraining role that it was intended to serve. If FISA courts have not only rubber-stamped administration requests but expanded the administration's authority to undertake surveillance without a warrant, then a FISA-like court for drones would not necessarily provide meaningful checks on the government's decision about targets.

The executive's preferred form of legal oversight is within the executive branch: in the president's words, "the establishment of an independent oversight board in the executive branch."[62] Along similar lines, in February 2013, Reuters reported that, according to anonymous US officials, despite their growing "political currency," Congress or the Obama Administration are unlikely to establish drone courts. Citing

Congressional aides, Reuters also reported that "discussions are at a preliminary stage, with officials also reviewing proposals that law professors have floated in academic studies."[63] Lastly, "even if a special court were established, however, congressional and administration officials said it would not happen quickly."[64]

The proposed alternative of a robust review process within the executive branch, however, would not appreciably remedy the question of checks and balances that has prompted calls for judicial branch review.[65] By many accounts,[66] the executive branch is already engaged in a rigorous discussion of targeting decisions; adding an additional layer of debate within the executive would not address the concern about checks and balances outside the executive branch. The main adjudicator, according to some proposals, would consist of senior advisors to the president, who could not produce objective, unbiased judgments because these advisors are also the president's most loyal lieutenants. Insofar as the spirit of the democratic peace argument deals with international ambitions, then judicial review would exclude the targets that have guided the overwhelming majority of American drone strikes.

Discussion and conclusion

This chapter has demonstrated how shielding the public from the costs of warfare has reduced domestic political checks on the use of drones. Drones are part of a larger political phenomenon in which the public has minimal incentives to restrict leaders' wartime powers because citizens have few direct and personal reminders of the cost of those wars. Without such constraints, leaders have little incentive to bring a close to wars abroad. The result is a global battlefield, largely without spatial or temporal constraints. If, as Obama argued, the use of drones instead of boots on the ground means that the president does not need Congressional authorization for the use of force, and if drones are domestically popular, then there are few barriers to the initiation and continuation of force. Institutional checks typically brought about by the use of conventional force – Congressional oversight given the deployment of troops or risk of fatalities – also fall by the wayside.

In presenting our argument above, the chapter has implicitly minimized the domestic implications of drone use against Americans or on American soil. This choice does not suggest that the constitutional rights are not important. As Steve Coll pointed out, the president's assertion that drones may target Americans who allegedly pose a terrorist threat if capture is not feasible is the "first instance in American history of a sitting president speaking of his intent to kill a particular US citizen without that citizen having been charged formally with a crime or convicted at trial."[67] Our point is that the near obsession with the constitutionality of killing American citizens – which has happened just a handful of times – ignores the bigger question for war and peace: the role of drones in targeting individuals abroad.

In the words of Michael Walzer, "No government will send young men into battle to kill and be killed without offering some justification for what they are doing."[68] The contrapositive risks become the case with the rise of drone warfare: when wars can be fought without young men and women going into battle to kill and being killed, governments do not have to offer a justification for what they are doing. This will undermine peace and liberal democracies. Ironically, the pressure from a democratic electorate to protect itself from the harms of warfare will not encourage policy makers to adopt peaceful or democratic methods – which Kant believed it would – but rather methods of warfare that leverage technology in order to insulate citizen-soldiers from harm. The irony is this insulation creates the possibility that leaders will no longer, in a prudential sense, have to obtain popular permission to go to war.

This response represents the pyrrhic victory of the advent of drone warfare. Wars involving drones will not risk US soldiers, and this is undoubtedly desirable, but in eschewing these risks, leaders will neither be bound by public consent for these actions nor will they be obligated to call these actions acts of war. Leaders will not seek public support for initiating or continuing war, rationalizing this circumvention on the basis that the nation's citizens are not in harm's way, even if this means citizens of other countries are in danger.

The point is not that more US troops should be put in harm's way. Rather, the development of drone warfare has given rise to the following paradox: US citizens are wary of domestic adversity and favor the candidate and policy that will minimize the costs of particular foreign policies. Leaders respond to these mandates by reducing these costs imposed on the electorate. They can do this either by adopting peaceful strategies or belligerent ones that are the least costly, such as using drones. The United States risks trending toward this second option. In so doing, however, leaders insulate implications about the war from the electorate, eliminating one of the factors that used to ensure ample oversight of war powers and limits on the reach of military force abroad.

CHAPTER FOUR

Drones and International Law

In March 2013, NBC News obtained a leaked version of the Obama Administration's classified White Paper on targeted killings. The document offered a legal justification for the use of drones to attack suspected militants; while it focused on American citizens, the paper's references to international law implied an extension of its argument to non-Americans. According to the administration, targeting leaders of al-Qaeda or associated forces is legal as an act of "national self-defense under international law." The document joins the Justice Department's "parade" of legal justifications for the drone policy proffered by senior administration officials, including Legal Advisor to the State Department Harold Koh in 2010 and Attorney General Eric Holder in 2012.[1] This chapter subjects these legal arguments to careful scrutiny, examining whether the use of drones is compatible with international legal commitments. In many cases, we conclude that the present-day use of combat drones is not consonant with international law, including the defense of territorial sovereignty and laws of armed conflict that seek to protect non-combatants from the effects of war. This break from legal tradition suggests a clear course of action: international legal norms need to be reconsidered in light of the challenges that asymmetric warfare poses, and governments should modify drone policy to conform with international law.

Under the rubric of international law and the use of force, two crucial questions arise. The first is whether drones are consistent with *jus ad bellum* commitments, or the recourse to the use of force. That is, whether the use of drones in places where the United States is not officially at war – in other words, anywhere other than Afghanistan – violate international understandings of when it is acceptable to use force. The second question is whether the use of drones violates *jus in bello*, or the laws of war once states are involved in conflict. This chapter evaluates both issues, focusing first on *where* and *when* the United States has used drones (*jus ad bellum*) and then *how* it has used them in combat (*jus in bello*). We examine the arguments legal advisors in the Obama Administration have advanced to defend the use of drones in terms of *jus ad bellum* and *jus in bello*, while also highlighting counterarguments. Ultimately, we conclude that the Obama Administration's defense of drones goes beyond reasonable interpretation of international law governing the use of force. It is obvious that other military practices – such as conventional bombing – would be less acceptable than the use of drones and precision-guided munitions, but this fact should not be regarded as the legitimating stroke when it comes to drone technologies.

Especially after the killing of American citizen and alleged terrorist Anwar al-Awlaki in 2011, the question of targeting American citizens without due process has received considerable attention from the Obama Administration and its critics.[2] While an important question in its own right, this chapter focuses primarily on whether and how combat drones are compatible with international legal commitments. We focus on the totality of drone targets, rather than the small American subset, because the use of drones against non-Americans has far greater implications for war and peace. Consequently, the subject of this chapter, international law, is more germane than domestic constitutional law when considering the legality of the vast majority of drone strikes.

Do drones conform to international law?

As Figure 4.1 suggests, the number of international humani-tarian law-related treaties has increased over past decades, formalizing state obligations to conduct war in ways that limit the effects of armed conflict for humanitarian reasons. A number of theories of international law and international rela-tions assume that when rules become institutionalized, states are more likely to be socialized and shamed into compliance with international law or at least to frame their actions as con-sistent with legal standards.[3]

Indeed, since 1945, as international legal principles – for example, territorial sovereignty and the principles of distinc-tion and proportionality – became prevailing norms, the same states that bombed entire cities during World War II became attentive to the question of civilian casualties. In the 1991 Persian Gulf War, for example, US allies operated under an

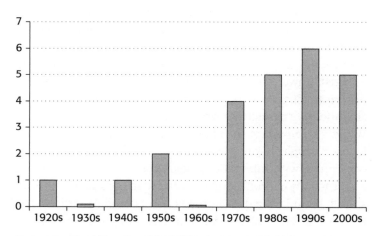

Source: International Committee of the Red Cross's customary IHL database

Figure 4.1 Number of international humanitarian law-related treaties per decade

"injunction to avoid high levels of civilian casualties,"[4] and they paid exhaustive attention to identifying and avoiding hospitals, historical sites, and religious facilities.[5] Such efforts exemplify a widespread desire to comply with the principle of distinction between civilian and military targets. Greater awareness of the distinction principle has coincided with technological developments that enable increasingly precise targeting. Far from bombing entire industrial valleys or cities, which would inevitably catch civilians in the crosshairs, new technology has allowed states to be far more discriminate. Indeed, the move to drones equipped with precision-guided munitions is the most recent improvement in that regard.

Against this backdrop, drones equipped with precision-guided munitions appear to offer a panacea. They are militarily useful yet ostensibly minimize civilian casualties, thereby allowing states to adhere to international legal commitments. In many respects, the legal and the strategic have become inextricable; as David Mets suggested, militaries pay "penalties of collateral damage" in the form of international censure and the wrath of the targeted population.[6] Technology, according to this argument, is helpful insofar as it can distinguish between military and civilian targets. Even the name for the weapons used on drones – "smart bombs" – speaks to the expectation that they will answer the twin demands of military utility and international norms. After all, as Air Force Lieutenant General Buster Glosson has written, "the objective has never been to see how many bombs we could drop, but to produce results."[7]

As further testament to the compliance pull of these norms on the use of force, the United States – and especially the Obama Administration, which has carried out the majority of US drone strikes – has gone to great lengths to defend its drone strikes as compatible with international law. In his 2010 keynote address to the American Society of

International Law, then-State Department Legal Advisor Koh stated: "It is the considered view of this Administration – and it has certainly been my experience during my time as Legal Adviser – that US targeting practices, including lethal operations conducted with the use of unmanned aerial vehicles, comply with all applicable law, including the laws of war."[8] This speech revealed the pressures on the administration to adhere to – or to be perceived as adhering to – its international legal commitments.

Nevertheless, American drone policy has come under growing scrutiny. A United Nations report on drones, for example, found that the United States had stretched the limits of international law in its targeting of terrorists in South Asia. In the conclusion of the report, the UN's Special Rapporteur on Extrajudicial, Summary or Arbitrary Executions, Phillip Alston, wrote that "there has been a highly problematic blurring and expansion of the boundaries of the applicable legal frameworks . . . [and] a tendency to expand who may permissibly be targeted and under what conditions."[9] The following sections review the competing positions on the grounds of *jus ad bellum*, the question of whom can be targeted and under what conditions, and whether the drone policy effectively distinguishes between civilians and combatants under the provisions of *jus in bello*. Having weighed arguments on both sides of the ledger, we retain reservations about the legality of the United States' use of drones, while also acknowledging the desirability of drones over more destructive uses of airpower like strategic bombing.

Jus ad bellum

The United Nations Charter, to which the United States is party, specifies two main circumstances under which states can use force in accordance with international law. First, states are authorized under Article 51 to use individual or collective self-defense. Second, states can use force if the UN Security Council has tendered its authorization.[10] Drones, then, are legal only under these two conditions. Barring such circumstances, Article 2(4), the nonintervention principle of the Charter, constrains states from using force in another territory.

Interpretations of Article 2(4) tend to divide into two camps, the restrictionists, who narrowly delimit the conditions under which states can use force legally, and counter-restrictionists, who have a more liberal reading.[11] The restrictionists construe the language of Article 2(4) – "All Members shall refrain in their international relations from the threat or use of force against the territorial integrity or political independence of any state" – as limiting almost any type of intervention. Counter-restrictionists, in contrast, have a more permissive view of the circumstances under which intervention is legal, citing both the "right of humanitarian intervention in customary international law"[12] and a broad reading of Article 51 that allows for preemptive self-defense.[13]

Prevailing interpretations of *jus ad bellum* organize around these two views. The counter-restrictionist position maintains that drone strikes are consistent with nonintervention principles. As Koh, noted, the United States is involved in an ongoing armed conflict with al-Qaeda and the Taliban that started with the 9/11 attacks.[14] As such, the United States is justified in using force against individuals suspected of terrorist affiliation regardless of their location. Moreover, Koh argued, such targeted killings are legally sanctioned as acts of anticipatory self-defense intended to prevent future attacks by militants. Indeed, legal scholars such as Robert Chesney point to a "continuous threat model" in which "a terrorist attack triggered Article 51 and . . . the resulting right to use force remains in effect over time insofar as the perpetrating organization intends to strike again."[15]

More recently, the administration's leaked White Paper on targeting decisions reaffirmed the legality under international law of targeting any senior leader of al-Qaeda or associated forces "who poses an imminent threat of violent attack against the United States." Throughout the paper, the government points to the principle of anticipatory self-defense – against an "imminent" threat – as justification for pursuing suspected terrorists outside "'hot' battlefields like Afghanistan."[16] The government does not rest its case there, however; the paper also relies heavily on the executive authority granted under the Authorization for Use of Military Force (AUMF). According to the AUMF: "The President has authority under the Constitution to take action to deter and prevent acts of international terrorism against the United States." The AUMF offers no temporal or spatial limits on the executive's ability to target suspected terrorists who "continue to pose an unusual and extraordinary threat to the national security and foreign policy of the United States."[17]

The restrictionist view, which we find more convincing, opposes the use of drones for targeting suspected terrorists outside "hot" battlefields on several grounds. First, according to international law, the recourse to force must respond to state-on-state attack, whereas non-state groups perpetrate terrorist attacks. As Mary Ellen O'Connell noted, "in at least five separate decisions spanning a sixty-year period, the [International Court of Justice] has said that the armed attack must be attributable to a state for the exercise of self-defense on that state's territory to be lawful."[18] Since targets in places like Pakistan, Yemen, and Somalia are allegedly part of terrorist groups, which are not states, uses of force against them would not be considered legal under international law.

Second, even if the terrorist groups were state-sponsored, the United States would have to be in a continuous conflict with the state sponsors for the use of force to be legal under international law. O'Connell observes that the United States is not engaged in an armed conflict with Pakistan, Yemen, and Somalia, which would rule out the legality of drone strikes in these countries. Even in Afghanistan, according to O'Connell, the act of self-defense arguably ended in 2002 when the Afghans set up their own government, after which the United States has assisted the Afghan government with its counter-insurgency efforts, rather than prosecuting the original, legally authorized war of self-defense.

Third, the restrictionist view contends that the notion of anticipatory self-defense does not apply in the case of drone strikes because they do not meet a reasonable standard of imminence. Anticipatory means that an impeding attack must be "instant, overwhelming, and leaving no choice of means, and no moment of deliberation."[19] While the US government suggests that terrorist targets constitute "a continuing, imminent threat" to the American people, it does not define "imminent" and international legal scholars have questioned whether many targeted militants would have qualified even under a liberal definition of imminence. Many of the targets that have been attacked outside combat zones are lower-level foot soldiers – just 2 percent are "high-level targets"[20] – who are "neither presently aggressing nor temporally about to aggress."[21] The characters on the "kill list" may be unsavory, but usually their actions are not sufficient to legitimate an act of anticipatory self-defense. Moreover, to meet the self-defense standard, it is incumbent upon the government to show how these individuals are culpable; however, to date, the government has offered only assertions that drone strikes are consistent with the UN Charter's provisions for self-defense.[22]

As this restrictionist view of *jus ad bellum* implies, the concern with drone strikes does not indict the drone technology itself but rather, as Jane Mayer of the *New Yorker* suggests, "the parameters of the war in which they're being used."[23] While drones have brought a different form of scrutiny because they are a new technology, the *jus ad bellum* discussion would be substantively similar whether the technology were drones or B-52 bombers. The question is whether the United States is authorized to engage in armed attacks against these targets at all. The more restrictive interpretations of *jus ad bellum* conclude that the only place where drone attacks are plausibly legal is in Afghanistan, where the United States initiated a war of self-defense after the 9/11 attacks. Consequently, drone attacks are not legal in countries with which the United States is not in a declared conflict, such as Pakistan, Yemen, and Somalia. The next section turns to whether the use of drones is compatible with *jus in bello* principles and, in particular, the principles of distinction and proportionality.

We realize that the debate between counter-restrictionists and restrictionists hinges on threat assessment in an age of asymmetric warfare. Modern technology has granted non-state actors the power to threaten nation-states. Counter-restrictionists understand this danger and believe that it warrants a new interpretation of international law. We disagree, however, and believe that the latitude provided in the AUMF sets a dangerous precedent. Although a restrictionist interpretation of IHL hamstrings certain military action, it is preferable because it pressures the United States to respect long-standing norms of sovereignty. Looking to the future, with other countries acquiring armed drones, the United States benefits more from preserving international sovereignty norms than from eroding them.

Jus in bello

The United States' defense of drones as a legal instrument of war centers on its *jus in bello* claims.[24] In his 2010 speech about drones, Koh pointed to two relevant aspects of the laws of war – distinction and proportionality – and noted that "in my experience, the principles of distinction and proportionality that the United States applies are not just recited at meetings."[25] The origins of both principles lie in the just war tradition, which offered philosophical and ethical guidelines for the goals and conduct of war.[26] Beginning in the nineteenth century, states began codifying just war notions, treaties, and protocols; the move toward positivism subsequently resulted in modern international humanitarian law (IHL), which seeks to protect non-combatants from the effects of war. IHL does not proscribe war but, as Chesterman wrote, it provides "justification for taking up arms against the wicked."[27] Its guidelines seek to strike a "balance between humanitarian concerns and the military requirements of States."[28] Among other things, IHL expects states to differentiate between civilians and combatants, and to ensure that the incidental damage to civilians be proportional to the military advantage. In the following sections, we address both of these principles in relation to the use of drones in combat.

Distinction[29]

The principle of distinction prohibits direct attacks against civilians. According to Article 48 of the Protocol Additional to the Geneva Convention (AP I, 1977), "In order to ensure respect for and protection of the civilian population and civilian objects, the Parties to the conflict shall at all times distinguish between the civilian population and combatants and between civilian objects and military objectives and accordingly shall direct their operations only against military objectives."[30] To act in accordance with this principle, the attacker must differentiate between those who are directly involved in hostilities and those who, according to Article 3 of the Geneva Conventions, are "taking no active part in the hostilities."[31]

This definition of distinction between combatant and civilian raises at least three issues of interpretation. First, in wartime, how does one distinguish between combatants and civilians? Article 4 of the Third Geneva Convention deals with the status of protected persons and their associated rights as prisoners of war,[32] and it also sets the groundwork for Article 50 of the Additional Protocol, which defines civilians in relation to Article 4 of the Third Geneva Convention.[33] The language points to challenges in the determination of civilian and combatant status when making targeting decisions, particularly in an asymmetric setting. According to Article 4, an individual can be considered a combatant and can become eligible for prisoner-of-war status under the following conditions:

(1)   that of being commanded by a person responsible for his subordinates;
(2)   that of having a fixed distinctive emblem recognizable at a distance;
(3)   that of carrying arms openly; and
(4)   that of conducting their operations in accordance with the laws and customs of war.

In World War II, application of these criteria was relatively straightforward. Combatants wore uniforms; civilians generally stayed in residential areas; and combatants fought for states party to international law. In a less conventional counterterrorism or counter-insurgency setting, it is far more difficult to determine if an individual has combatant or civilian status. In other words, irregular warfare intensifies the "identification problem,"[34] that is, knowing who is an enemy combatant and who is not. Actors involved in hostilities often wear civilian clothing rather than "distinctive emblems recognizable at a distance." Combatants, moreover, may not conduct operations in accordance with international law, especially if they are not fighting for states that are parties to international legal conventions.[35]

A second, related challenge involves judging whether individuals are direct participants in combat, and therefore legitimate targets, or indirect participants, and therefore protected civilians. As the battlefield has become more integrated with population centers, civilians experience an "increased intermingling"[36] with combatants. Distinctions become blurred across both time and space, with a "revolving door" between active involvement in combat and civilian nonparticipation,[37] as well as spatial intermingling of combatants and civilians.[38] This intermingling facilitates the involvement of civilians in hostilities, and creates a functional similarity between combatants and those who take some part in the hostilities. For example, both combatants and civilians can collect intelligence. Yet, whereas combatants are always legitimate targets in an area of armed conflict, civilians are targetable only "for such time" as they are engaged in hostilities. This means that some civilians are legitimate targets intermittently.[39]

In 2009, the International Committee of the Red Cross (ICRC) convened nearly fifty experts to clarify the legal distinctions between direct and indirect participation in hostilities and between legal and illegal targets. After a series of meetings, the ICRC issued guidelines on *The Interpretive Guidance on the Notion of Direct Participation in Hostilities under IHL*, which proposed that "direct causation should be understood as meaning that the harm in question must be brought about in one causal step."[40] The legal standing of some activities, such as firing missiles and operating a vehicle's remote control, is clear-cut. Yet, the ICRC acknowledged that, ultimately, "the difference between 'direct' and 'indirect' participation can be difficult to establish."[41] Although the "one causal step" standard sought to elucidate this issue, most activities are excluded from this designation.[42] Recruitment, for example, is a two-step process, as is augmenting the capacity of one party to the conflict.

Despite the ICRC's efforts, international consensus on

the participation standard remains elusive. According to Ohlin, "the direct participation standard is difficult to apply to terrorists, and there is currently little uniform state practice that would shed light on the content of the alleged customary norm."[43] According to the Israeli High Court of Justice Judgment on Targeted Killings, "the 'direct' character of the part taken should not be narrowed merely to the person committing the physical act of attack" but should also include those people who collect intelligence, transport combatants so they can engage in hostilities, and use hostile weapons. The Court concluded that "the notion of direct participation in hostilities is complex, emotive, and still inadequately resolved."[44] The United States has considered material support to terrorists in violation of international law, but this too is an ambiguous standard: financial aid to terrorists would be a considered material support, yet it is "a far cry from a *direct* participation in hostilities."[45]

Indeed, major conceptual issues remain unresolved. Even if "direct" participation were to have a straightforward definition, which it does not, how does one deal with the issue of momentary and intermittent involvement? Does a single instance of direct participation mean that an individual is a legitimate target? And if an individual ceases to participate in hostilities, at what point does he or she regain legal protection? Such questions lack simple and obvious answers.[46]

A third challenge falls under the heading of "military objectives." Article 52(2) of AP I defines military objectives as "limited to those objects which by their nature, location, purpose or use make an effective contribution to military action and whose total or partial destruction, capture or neutralization, in the circumstances ruling at the time, offers a definite military advantage." As Dinstein notes, Article 52(2) "does not produce a workable acid test for such verification with targeting only those objectives that produce military advantages."[47]

Within this legal framework, some attacks patently violate the principle of distinction. The strategic bombing that the Allies undertook in World War II – in which they carpeted entire cities with bombs – would be illegal under contemporary international law. Not only did the attackers take few precautions to avoid civilian casualties, but they intentionally targeted civilians in the hope that the civilians would convince their governments to acquiesce.[48] Further, "some Allied officers thought the raids in eastern Germany might serve the additional purpose of impressing the Soviet Union" because, by this stage in the war, fissures were appearing between the USSR and its Anglo-American allies.[49]

Despite a few clear-cut scenarios, the meanings of combatant status and military objectives are largely subject to interpretation. The ambiguity of the Convention's language is, in one sense, an asset. States are more likely to ratify provisions whose compliance is difficult to verify.[50] Moreover, the ambiguity provides flexibility and a "built-in ability to anticipate future scenarios" by not locking in specific legal language.[51] Nonetheless, the ambiguous legal language also means that actors can more easily argue that they are in compliance with international law. As Antonio Cassese points out, the language is "so sweeping that it can cover practically anything."[52] Almost any wartime targeting can be justified under this definition because almost any facility can plausibly be used for military purposes.

The lack of a clear litmus test becomes especially problematic given recent asymmetric conflicts, where individuals tend to fall along a spectrum of involvement. At one end of the spectrum is a man firing a gun; at the other end is a civilian playing no role in the attack. In between is a continuum of cases varying by the level of involvement in, or support for, an attack. While radioing in directions to a mortar team is probably sufficient to render one a combatant (whether armed or not), other cases are not so easy – for instance, civilians who merely warn the mortar crew that Americans are coming, civilians who provide food or water to the crew, or those who merely give the crew words of support. As the ICRC and Israeli High Court have suggested, placing individuals on the continuum is often a challenging, nuanced question.

The interrelated questions of the age, agency, and accountability of suspected combatants only exacerbate the moral ambiguity of targeting decisions. David Bellavia recounts an incident in the Iraq War in which the Mahdi Militia in Iraq used a small child of five or six as a forward observer. Even though there was no doubt about the boy's role as a facilitator of attacks on Americans, US soldiers declined to target the child on moral grounds. As Bellavia and Bruning explained, "Nobody wants a child on his conscience."[53] Moreover, the age problem presents even more shades of grey. At what age does a person become sufficiently morally accountable to be a legitimate target? It is unlikely that any *a priori* rule can cover such situations; the ability to respond flexibly and contextually to such ambiguity is a reflection of the human capacity to exercise moral judgment in complex situations.

To be sure, humans remain integral to the drone-targeting process since we are not talking about the fully autonomous "killer robots" decried by anti-war movements.[54] Nonetheless, when drone advocates suggest that technology has made drone targeting more precise, they seem to conflate drones' ability to hit a target precisely with drones' ability to minimize casualties. For example, former Prosecutor of the International Criminal Court Luis Moreno-Ocampo concluded in his report on coalition targeting in Iraq, "nearly 85 percent of weapons released by UK aircraft were precision-guided, a figure which would tend to corroborate effort to minimize casualties."[55] Similarly, the US military's *Joint Vision 2010* asserted that "in all operations technological advances . . . allow them [the war fighters] to make better decisions." These technologies may provide militaries with more information with which to distinguish a combatant from a civilian. They may also allow militaries to pinpoint and target some individuals, while sparing others. The weapons do not, however, ensure that a selected target is a legitimate target. The fog of war inevitably implies ambiguities which technological solutions cannot eliminate. Indeed, the very question of evidentiary standards for the use of lethal force is itself a matter of normative judgment. Targeting determinations are thus of a legal and ethical, rather than technological, nature. For all that technology can do to improve human life, there is no reason at present to believe that it can eliminate the fog of war.

Finally, the definition of collateral damage deserves attention in the context of the distinction principle. In discussions of drones and collateral damage, a disconcerting ambiguity has surfaced in press releases and, more disturbingly, in legal briefings, military manuals, and perhaps the minds of most drone operators. Over the past decade, modern military manuals have employed two very different definitions of collateral damage. The first definition is a factual one: collateral damage refers to unintended damage or loss of life. As a 1998 USAF Intelligence target guide laid out, collateral damage refers to *"unintended destruction* suffered by opposition, neutral or friendly parties."[56] This definition turns only on the emphasized phrase "unintended destruction." With this definition in mind, it seems accurate to say that drones limit collateral damage since these technologies allow for the more accurate targeting of intended targets. This is just a question of technological precision and says nothing about the normative (legal or ethical) judgment that was made prior to the determination of what was intended or unintended in a strike. But after the Iraq invasion in 2003, there was subtle slippage in this definition toward more normative standards of collateral damage.

In a 2008 Pentagon manual, the term "collateral damage" is defined as "Unintentional or incidental injury or damage to persons or objects *that would not be lawful military targets in the circumstances ruling at the time.*"[57] This definition of collateral damage is more expansive and, in addition to question of intention, turns on the italicized passage concerning "lawful military targets." This is a very different type of definition of collateral damage that carries with it the normative weight of law and morality. Here, it would not be accurate to say that "drones limit collateral damage" since the technology of drones does not *necessarily* allow strategists or operators to make more judicious normative judgments concerning "lawful military targets." In this second case, we risk confusing technological precision for precision in human judgment. These are not the same and, as outlined in the next chapter, there is good reason to be wary of this conflation.

Proportionality[58]
Closely linked with the principle of distinction between military and civilian objects is the principle of proportionality. If an action is proportional, anticipated military gain must exceed the anticipated damage to civilians and their property. Article 51(5)(b) of AP I proscribes "an attack which may be expected to cause incidental loss of civilian life, injury to civilians, damage to civilian objects, or a combination thereof, which would be excessive in relation to the concrete and direct military advantage anticipated."[59]

When assessing whether war crimes occurred in the context of the 2003 Iraq War – specifically, during the combat phase between March and May – ICC Prosecutor Moreno-Ocampo offered his views on this legal principle. He noted:

> The death of civilians during an armed conflict, no matter how grave and regrettable, does not in itself constitute a war crime. International humanitarian law (IHL), international

> law that applies to armed conflicts, and the Rome Statute of
> the International Criminal Court permit belligerents to carry
> out proportionate attacks against military objectives, even
> when it is known that some civilian deaths or injuries will
> occur.[60]

In other words, the incidental or unintentional killing of civilians is permitted under international law; however, harm to civilians that clearly exceeds the anticipated military advantage – that is, disproportionate harm – is proscribed.

Article 8(2)(b)(iv) of the 1998 Rome Statute clarifies the 1977 AP I principle of proportionality and requires an assessment of the following: (a) the anticipated civilian damage or injury; (b) the anticipated military advantage; and (c) whether (a) was "clearly excessive" in relation to (b). While this calculus may sound straightforward, the determination is quite subjective. A soldier determines military advantage "based on his or her experience and evaluation of the target in the context of the entire campaign, and the information reasonably available at the relevant time."[61] Unless civilian fatalities are the result of intentional targeting – that is, the commander had access in advance to information that would show the likelihood of such an outcome – and those fatalities exceed military benefit, then the attacker is not in violation of international law. Akin to the demands of the principle of distinction, states are required, under Article 57 of AP I, to "do everything feasible" to anticipate harm to civilians and to ensure that the military advantage exceeds civilian damage.

Members of the policy and legal communities have lengthily debated whether drone strikes meet standards of proportionality. Unfortunately, as Walzer notes, in scholars' discussions of proportionality, often "'disproportionate' violence . . . is simply violence they don't like, or it is violence committed by people they don't like." A more tractable approach to assessing proportionality leverages data to compare pre-operational estimates of civilian deaths with the total killed by drone strikes. These rates vary dramatically, from a total of about 17% according to the New America Foundation (between 2004 and 2011), to 23.85% according to the Bureau of Investigative Journalism, to 3.86% according to the UMASS Drone project.[62] According to Avery Plaw, the data suggest that strikes have killed between three and nineteen times more military targets than civilians; Daniel Byman observed that these strikes have eliminated key al-Qaeda and Taliban leaders who are difficult to replace.[63] On this basis, commentators such as Plaw have concluded "that the issue of proportionality does not appear to provide a basis for claiming that US drone strikes in general are either unethical or illegal."[64]

Other estimates are less charitable toward the government. Kilcullen and Exum cited different statistics to argue that the use of drones in targeted and signature strikes violate proportionality standards: "Press reports suggest that over the last three years drone strikes have killed about 14 terrorist leaders. But, according to Pakistani sources, they have also killed some 700 civilians. This is 50 civilians for every militant killed, a hit rate of 2 percent – hardly 'precision.'"[65] Mary Ellen O'Connell's work, referenced earlier, has focused on the way in which drone strikes cause widespread and disproportionate harms. At one point, she describes a particularly problematic military strike that caused "the disproportionate loss of civilian lives. . . . Fifty civilians killed for one intended target is a disproportionate result by anyone's calculation."[66]

Plaw has suggested that engaging, and perhaps settling, this seemingly abstract debate over proportionality comes down to the concrete process of "counting the dead."[67] We believe that Plaw is partially correct, but that this debate also turns on interpreting the numbers – which, for a number of reasons, is extremely difficult to do. Indeed, that the percentages vary so widely is itself telling since it reflects different ways in which civilians are counted as militants by some groups and as civilians by others. Many cases are ambiguous, with press reports referring to "people killed" or "unknown" status, making it difficult to know whether to put those individuals in the numerator (civilian) or denominator (total). The US government's practice of avoiding comment on the specifics of drone strikes – while also lauding their effectiveness – makes it even harder to resolve these debates.

In many ways, this debate hinges on how we evaluate the "denominator" of the proportionality calculation. If the amount of civilian damage relative to the overall military advantage is the pivotal consideration, then what we consider to be the military advantage is critical. Thus, casting military objectives in expansive terms, such as eliminating evil or fighting terror, becomes so broad that any civilian damage is, by comparison, more palatable. "Evil" is, by definition, something that should be destroyed. If a modern military is charged with the eradication of great evil, then the use of any military means may appear justified. In the wake of the attacks of September 11, George Bush repeatedly expressed his intention to round up terrorists on the grounds that these actors were evil. But as Walzer noted, this "round-up of the aggressors will most often require a military conquest, and conquest has effects that reach far beyond the people who are rounded up."[68]

While the Obama Administration sought to distance itself from the language of Bush's global war on terror (GWOT), the successor policy has pursued an equally expansive military objective, failing to rectify the confusion over proportionality. When the transfer of US forces from Iraq to Afghanistan accelerated in the fall of 2009, the Obama Administration ceased describing operations in terms of the "global war on terror."[69] The phrase was seen as too ideological, too broad, too ambiguous, and too likely to combine disparate groups under the common term "terrorist." Instead, the administration used the phrase "overseas contingency operation" (OCO). This shift in language, seemingly technocratic, avoided lumping loosely related belligerents together under a single heading. The adoption of OCO language also appeared to narrow the goals of military operations. Rather than large-scale invasions, OCOs respond to the emergence of contingent targets with so-called "surgical" strikes executed without a declaration of war.

Nevertheless, OCO and GWOT may represent a distinction without difference; both policies are fraught with concerns about the appropriate means to achieve ends of such great proportions.[70] Contingency can refer to something that happens by chance or to an occurrence that is uncertain. OCO thus connotes military operations that aim at potential threats to national security, but that have not yet been actualized. In practice, this policy entails targeting non-state actors, small groups, and individuals who are planning attacks on the United States. The Obama Administration employed this logic to justify the drone attack in Yemen that killed Anwar al-Awlaki in September 2011, even though the United States was not at war with Yemen and the target was an American citizen who had not been convicted of a crime.[71] The moral and legal difficulties of targeting "contingencies" are therefore very similar to those experienced in targeting "evil." Evil is ubiquitous and can hide anywhere; contingency targets are similarly boundless.

Of course, maintaining an appropriate balance between the objectives of military campaigns and the means by which we achieve these objectives is not as easy as it sounds. This challenge is particularly acute during times of rapid technological innovation. Walzer, who remains deeply critical of US targeting practices, identifies the danger of inverting the norm of proportionality:

> Proportionality is a matter of adjusting means to ends, but as the Israeli philosopher Yehuda Melzer has pointed out, there is an overwhelming tendency in wartime to adjust ends to means instead, that is to redefine initially narrow goals in order to fit the available military forces and technologies . . . It is necessary in such arguments to hold ends constant, but how does one do that? In practice, the inflation of ends is probably inevitable unless it is barred by considerations of justice itself.[72]

Walzer's point, which we find apt, reduces to a straightforward insight: when given more precise military scalpels, there is a good chance that everything will look like it deserves surgical removal. Furthermore, the size of diagnosed tumors is likely to correlate with the size of the scalpel. "Available military forces and technologies" will skew determinations of proportionality; avoiding miscalculation will depend on "considerations of justice itself."[73] These considerations, however, are put in jeopardy by technologies that shield troops from the harm that they often faced in traditional military confrontations.

In the eyes of many ethicists and legal theorists, like Walzer, minimizing one's own casualties at the expense of those on the opposing side can constitute a substantial transgression. For example, Walzer cautions to take great care in avoiding civilian casualties. He writes that "even if the target is very important and the number of innocent people threatened relatively small, [military planners] must risk soldiers before they kill civilians."[74] Walzer calls not only for careful technical and legal assessments when decisions are reached about targeting, but for real sacrifices and risks on the part of military personnel as they strive to protect civilians.[75] That soldiers have the ethical duty to risk themselves for the sake of the opposing side's civilians is not a popular point, especially on the home front. For example, ground operations that risk US troops but minimize civilian casualties might be more ethical than air strikes that accomplish similar goals but risk civilian lives. Walzer reaches this conclusion because he considers just war doctrine to be a doctrine of "radical responsibility" in which political and military leaders must attend to, and be willing to sacrifice, their "own people" as well as the civilians of the "other side."[76]

Elsewhere, Walzer and Avishai Margalit advise militaries to provide the following guidance to soldiers: "By wearing a uniform, you take on yourself a risk that is borne only by those who have been trained to injure others . . . as a soldier, you are asked to take an extra risk for the sake of limiting the scope of war. Combatants are the Davids and Goliaths of their communities. You are our David."[77]

Their outlook is not universally shared. Asa Kasher and Amos Yadlin, for example, contend that by operating in the vicinity of civilians, "terrorists" excuse their opponents from the responsibility that Walzer and Margalit identify. According to Kasher and Yadlin, "jeopardizing combatants rather than bystanders during a military act against a terrorist would mean shouldering responsibility for the mixed nature of the vicinity."[78] In their opinion, contemporary conflict settings that intermingle civilians and combatants make it prohibitively difficult and even unreasonable to adopt Walzer and Margalit's principle. Interestingly, many experts in counter-insurgency, including General David Petraeus and the authors of the 2006 army counter-insurgency (COIN) field manual, suggest that there are practical reasons to support Walzer's philosophical claims. According to the COIN manual, winning the "hearts and minds" of a foreign civilian population requires minimizing civilian casualties: "Ultimate success in COIN is gained by protecting the populace, not the COIN force. If military forces remain in their compounds, they lose touch with the people, appear to be running scared, and cede the initiative to the insurgents. Aggressive saturation patrolling, ambushes, and listening post operations must be conducted, risk shared with the populace, and contact maintained."[79] Or, as the manual summarizes: "sometimes, the more you protect your force, the less secure you may be."[80] Such protection of civilians introduces a paradox. To protect the populace, soldiers will need to leave their garrisons. At least in the short term, being exposed will likely incur more casualties, even if it provides practical benefits and a more ethical/legal way of protecting the populace. Here, we reach an irony that may bear on the future of IHL. If troop losses increase, due to increased exposure on the ground, will the principle of proportionality be more adequately satisfied? This seems likely. As the number of troop casualties increases, will there be a corresponding domestic blowback against the conflict? This also seems very likely. The perceptions of war on the home front (and, indirectly, the domestic politics that correspond to these perceptions) may put pressure on leaders to withdraw from conflicts where an effort to satisfy proportionality norms leads to one's own casualties. Thus, wars that comply with IHL, or more generally with the spirit of the just war tradition, may be highly unpopular ones and perhaps wars that end as draws. This is to reframe a position set forth in the previous chapter: one of the long-standing backstops against military aggression is the democratic accountability that leaders and strategists consider in authorizing military activity. The greater the cost borne by a democratic populace, the less popular a conflict will be. But in the drone age, democratic citizens' risk aversion may encourage leaders to select ineffective or illegitimate strategies – rather than seeking peace.

Conclusion

This chapter has evaluated the use of drones from the perspective of international law, focusing on questions of *jus ad bellum* and *jus in bello*. We argue that two flawed assumptions belie the argument that advancements in technology help make "better decisions." The first is that technology can differentiate between combatants and innocents – a distinction that is central to international humanitarian law. In asymmetric settings, such distinctions are fraught with ambiguity and cannot be satisfactorily answered by sophisticated technology, but rather by serious legal and ethical discussions. Few would deny that individuals who plant bombs in Afghan villages are legitimate military targets. But the legitimacy of many other targets, as the ICRC found in its meetings of legal experts, is not as clear-cut. The definition of participation (either direct or indirect) in hostilities and the statute of limitations on individuals' past participation are legal and moral questions that are embedded within, but not resolved by, the use of drone technology.

A second flawed assumption is that technology can set limits on such ambitious goals as "eradicating evil." As we have noted, assessing proportionality in the best of cases poses problems, given the difficulties of distinguishing combatant from civilian and of anticipating military advantage relative to civilian damage. When goals are cast in such open-ended ways, military advantage can encompass almost anything and can justify almost anything as a proportional measure.

We should note that there are many ways in which military personnel have used drones to gather better intelligence. This capability is no doubt useful in upholding the principles of distinction and proportionality and we do not mean to suggest otherwise. We do, however, want to underscore that the mere use of particular technologies in military strikes cannot bestow on them legal and ethical legitimacy; it is individuals – rather than technologies alone – who make these assessments. The arguments in this chapter are meant to serve as warnings against overstating the legal and ethical progress made recently in the conduct of war. They are also meant to guard us against moral smugness, which tends to breed complacency. In security studies, it is often said that a misplaced sense of security is the greatest danger. Likewise, a misplaced sense of moral legitimacy can lead to a dangerous lack of vigilance about ethical and legal matters.

As we suggest, some of the debate about whether drones are compatible with international law arises because of the technology itself. Drones equipped with precision munitions raise important questions about the *jus in bello* principles of distinction and proportionality, given the increasing and often unreflective use of these technologies. In this respect, one could argue that the notion that technology is apolitical and normatively neutral, as has been implied in the government's defense of drones, is a recent product of modernity and, specifically, American modernity. This idea allows one to think that using technology obviates ethical dilemmas. But here we argue the contrary: that technology is always political and value laden.[81] Fabricating and implementing technologies is an inherently ethical task. Recognizing this dynamic helps avoid fixation with the technical capabilities of military technologies and refocuses attention on the inability of these technologies to solve moral and legal dilemmas.

These legal dilemmas are embedded in, yet exist apart from, drone technology. Whether striking targets in places such as Pakistan, Yemen, and Somalia is legal would be a legitimate question, irrespective of the technique used. Perhaps the unmanned component gives a sense of plausible deniability – for both the host as well as the US government – since there are no American pilots flying the aircraft. However, the real question is whether the United States can still predicate these strikes on post-9/11 counterterrorism arguments. The indeterminacy of the culpability of targets, coupled with the open-ended – both in time and space – nature of the strikes, makes for a flimsy basis for *jus ad bellum*. It also establishes a precedent that will legitimize similar behavior by other states that are developing armed drones and will presumably seek to use them in the future. We return to this question of precedent in the conclusion of the book.

CHAPTER FIVE

The Ethics of Drone Warfare

This chapter focuses on the ethics of using unmanned aerial vehicles in targeted killings and signature strikes. In the opening chapter of this volume, we addressed the problem of "dirty hands," a situation in which a politically expedient strategy involves violating certain moral or legal norms. Today, in the age of asymmetric threats, the issue of "dirty hands" has become much more pressing. With increasing frequency, leaders who negotiate asymmetric conflict will have to make political and military actions that risk running askance of ethical guidelines; some of these actions will involve the use of semiautonomous and autonomous weapon systems. While "dirty hands" are a problem as old as Augustine, acknowledging the problem is not tantamount to sanctioning moral messiness. Even in a world fraught with ambiguity, there are certain acts – political and militarily – that should be prohibited. Our task in this chapter, therefore, is to clarify the moral questions at the heart of drone warfare so that policy makers and military planners can keep their hands as clean as possible.

Many scholars have looked at the promise and pitfalls of just war theory in terms of contemporary warfare, and specifically of the US policy of targeted killings, and this work is extremely valuable.[1] On the whole, however, these attempts have gotten ahead of themselves by turning attention to specific tenets of the laws of war, primarily distinction and proportionality, while not considering more basic philosophical questions that attend the proliferation of modern military technologies. In short, they tend to skip over the way that our understanding of technology and its expedience might skew our normative judgments about the moral and legal dimensions of combat drones. In this chapter, we encourage the reader to take a step back from the immediate legal concerns posed by drones and to consider a broader philosophical critique of modern military technologies and the way they affect the changing character of warfare. These points of ethical theory are often glossed over, but this oversight demonstrates the problem with the current discourse surrounding drones – that sustained ethical reflection about the changing nature of warfare is set aside in the name of expediency.

To this point in the book, we have laid out the history, politics, and laws that define the drone debate. With the exception of the argument from chapter 3 on democratic accountability, and the last section of chapter 4, we have largely avoided making broad normative arguments about the way that one *should* think about drone warfare. There is, unfortunately, no easy answer to the question of drones and asymmetric warfare. This chapter does not pretend to provide an answer to whether, or in what cases, drones are morally obligatory. Instead, it explores a number of basic philosophical problems in thinking about the legitimacy of drones in armed combat, drawing on information provided in earlier chapters. We hope to provide a philosophical starting point for grappling with very difficult political and legal issues. This chapter on ethics of drones is not an afterthought, but rather an appeal to think again about the most basic assumptions about military technology and its relationship to warfare, with particular emphasis on unmanned aerial systems.

We reach a number of closely related conclusions in this chapter. In the first section, we argue that the use of drones in modern conflict poses what philosophers call "a moral hazard," a situation in which individuals are willing to take part in increasingly risky behaviors if they are shielded from the negative consequences of said behavior. In the second section, we suggest that drone operators and policy makers will face this moral hazard with increasing frequency and must be trained to negotiate the ethical responsibility entailed in this new form of warfare. Unfortunately, as we explain, this ethical training may be seen as superfluous or unnecessary in an age of what Herbert Marcuse termed "technological rationality" in which "the easy" is used interchangeably with "the good" or "the just." In the third section, we outline the moral dangers of targeted killings becoming banal and commonplace in the international community; this argument shifts the responsibility for the US drone campaign back onto the citizens who tacitly support it. Finally, we make two arguments against the "moral necessity" of combat drones, challenging a line of thinking that has recently emerged in the literature on military ethics, namely that the use of drones in combat should be regarded as obligatory.

The moral hazard of drones[2]

In developing an ethics of drone combat, clear decision procedures for military planners and soldiers would be convenient – the type that could guide them, automatically, unthinkingly, mechanically, to the right decision about drone use. Alas, ethics, philosophy, and humans do not work this way. The difference between humans and robots is precisely the ability to think and reflect; in Immanuel Kant's words, to set and pursue ends for themselves. And these ends cannot be set beforehand in some hard and fast way – even if Kant sometimes thought they could.[3] Consequently, we did not write this section on the ethics of war and peace and the moral hazard of military technologies in a manner appropriate to robots:

input decision procedure, output decision, and correlated action. Rather, we emphasize repeatedly the pointedly human character of ethical decisions and the hazard that one faces in ignoring this fact. It is this character that risks being forgotten in the hurry to enter the age of semiautonomous weapon systems. Moral decisions about drones require cautious deliberation, rather than speedy judgments.

In the coming decades, with the rise of advanced military technology such as drones, modern war fighters and the citizens that support them will have to think through the "moral hazard" implied by drone usage. Moral hazard is a concept common in economic and philosophical circles; it describes a situation in which a party engages in risky or morally questionable behaviors because he or she does not have to face the consequences of these actions. The history of the term "moral hazard" is a curious one. It originally had nothing to do with morality. It began as an insurance industry term referring to people's tendency to take greater risks when they do not face the associated costs. Once a car was insured, it was more likely to be driven recklessly; once cargo was insured, it was more likely to be transported through the Bermuda Triangle. Any costs incurred in such risky behavior could be passed off on the principle, the insurance company. In response, these companies sought clients who wouldn't, for any number of reasons, fall prey to these temptations. Identifying such individuals was no small task since it required screening for those who would act with caution and restraint even when given the latitude to do otherwise. Insurance agencies mitigated moral hazards by incentivizing good behavior by adjusting premiums and liabilities.

Governments and international institutions, however, have yet to adjust liabilities so as to incentivize good behavior with drones. Targeted killings and signature strikes have always been in the repertoire of military planners, but never, in the history of warfare, have they cost so very little to use. Historically, there have been significant risks associated with these types of military activities. First, a nation-state had to risk its soldiers or operatives. And if it risked the lives of soldiers, it risked public censure if these individuals were killed or captured. And if such a strike was successful and publicly endorsed, there was still the risk of retribution. Drones have allowed some governments to obviate most, if not all, of these costly risks. As US military forces acquire more autonomous drones and hire private security firms to operate them, these killings will become even less expensive for the American citizenry. This is a trend that soldiers and the citizens who support them have to confront head on. Paul Kahn's recent work on "riskless war" is particularly good on the ethical implications of avoiding the traditional costs of war.[4]

That technology makes life easier is one of the unquestioned shibboleths of the day. Modern medical devices make surgery a snap and airplanes and subways make transportation fast and cheap. But anyone who has gotten on the express train going the wrong way knows that there is a significant downside to speed and efficiency. To make life easier, the train has to be pointed in the right direction and the correct kidney needs to be painlessly removed. Since the technology itself does not delimit its wise or moral use, it is the job of decision makers to align it with our intellectual, or in President Obama's word, "moral," compasses. The question remains, however, of how we should orient these compasses. A first step is to guard against moral hazards.

Moral hazards have long concerned ethicists. While drones have become the weapons of our age, the moral dilemma that drone warfare presents is not new. In fact, it is very, very old. Plato was perhaps the first to articulate the problem and present it in the story of Gyges in his *Republic*.[5] We have included that allegory below so that you may consider the relationship between this ancient story and the present-day implications of drone technology. The relationship is not obvious, so it will serve as a sort of warm-up in thinking through the moral decision-making about drones. The story of Gyges is offered by one of Socrates' interlocutors in the following manner:

> According to the tradition, Gyges was a shepherd in the service of the king of Lydia; there was a great storm, and an earthquake made an opening in the earth at the place where he was feeding his flock. Amazed at the sight, he descended into the opening, where, among other marvels, he beheld a hollow brazen horse, having doors, at which he stooping and looking in saw a dead body of stature, as appeared to him, more than human, and having nothing on but a gold ring; this he took from the finger of the dead and reascended . . . Now the shepherds met together, according to custom, that they might send their monthly report about the flocks to the king; into their assembly he came having the ring on his finger, and as he was sitting among them he chanced to turn the collet of the ring inside his hand, when instantly he became invisible to the rest of the company and they began to speak of him as if he were no longer present. He was astonished at this, and again touching the ring he turned the collet outwards and reappeared; he made several trials of the ring, and always with the same result – when he turned the collet inwards he became invisible, when outwards he reappeared. Whereupon he contrived to be chosen one of the messengers who were sent to the court; where as soon as he arrived he seduced the queen, and with her help conspired against the king and slew him, and took the kingdom.[6]

This story of ethical egoism (in which self-interest and power serves as the justification for action) is as old as western ethics itself. Plato wants this story to illicit a certain response in his readers: the feeling of disgust. He hopes that a reader is taken aback by the way that practical efficiency takes the place of moral legitimacy. The fact that the technological feats of the ring allow Gyges to kill without getting caught does nothing to quell a reader's worries. In fact, it only adds to the moral apprehension. Even when it is incredibly easy, expediency is not necessarily virtue. This may be true, but the story also suggests that it is difficult to blame a person whom you can't see, and even harder to bring them to justice. In these disturbing cases, a wicked act can go unexamined and therefore unpunished. This story from the *Republic* suggests that any kingdom based on this sort of deception could not be a just one: under cover of night what else might transpire in such a kingdom?

One might argue that the myth of Gyges is a suitable allegory to describe the combatants who have attacked and killed American civilians and troops in the last ten years. A shepherd from the Middle East discovers that he has the power of invisibility, the power to strike a fatal blow against a more powerful adversary, the power to do so without getting caught, the power to benefit from his deception. These, after all, are the tactics of terrorism. However, we would like to suggest that the myth of Gyges is not a story about terrorism but a warning about the tactics of drone warfare. We believe there is a meaningful comparison between the myth and the moral dangers of employing drones to target suspected terrorists. What is striking about the tale of Gyges is the ease with which he can commit murder and get away scot-free. The technological advantage provided by the ring ends up serving as the justification for its use. Terrorists, whatever the moral value of their deeds, may be found and punished; as humans, they are subject to retribution, whether it is corporal or legal. They may lose or sacrifice their lives. They may, in fact, be killed in the middle of the night by a drone. Because remote-controlled machines cannot suffer these consequences, and the humans who operate them do so at a great distance, the myth of Gyges is a more trenchant parable of certain aspects of US counterterrorism.

The increased use of drones to target suspected terrorists has spurred an animated but incomplete debate about their use. Opponents have mostly limited their criticism to questions of legal and political precedent (as discussed in previous chapters): the prohibition against assassination; the importance of democratic accountability in preventing perpetual war; the legitimacy of using force in states with which the aggressor is not at war; and the delicate issue of proportionality.

Only recently has the debate shifted to important moral questions.[7] Perhaps, at first blush, the answers to these questions appear self-evident. What could be wrong with the use of unmanned aerial vehicles? After all, they limit the cost of war in terms of both blood and money. The US troops who operate them can maintain safer standoff positions in Eastern Europe or at home. And, according to Bradley Strawser and others discussed later in this chapter, armed with precision-guided munitions, these drones limit collateral damage and allow modern militaries to make finely tuned determinations concerning target selection. To quote former Secretary of Defense and Director of the CIA Leon Panetta, drones are "very precise and very limited in terms of collateral damage."[8] What, then, could be the moral concerns surrounding drones?

What we find unsettling is the idea that these facts about expediency could be confused for moral justification. Return, for a minute, to the moral disgust that Gyges evokes in us. Gyges also risked very little in attacking the king. The success of his mission was almost assured, thanks to the technological advantage of his ring. Gyges could sneak past the king's guards unscathed, so he did not need to kill anyone he did not intend on killing. Philosophers find the confusion between expediency and justification particularly abhorrent and guard against it with the only weapon they have: a distinction. The "fact–value distinction" holds that statements of fact should never be confused with statements of value. More strongly put, this distinction means that statements of fact do not even *imply* statements of value. "Can" does not imply "ought." To say that "we *can* target individuals without incurring troop casualties" does not imply that "we *ought* to target said individuals." This seems obvious – but when Obama responded that continued US military strikes in the Middle East did not constitute a violation of the War Powers Resolution because they did not risk American casualties,[9] he came close to suggesting that the justification of these strikes rested solely on their ease and the relative safety of US troops. Our concern is that the ring of Gyges has the power to obscure the obvious.

War by remote control[10]

Moving from ancient ethical allegories to contemporary history: ten years ago, we watched the Iraq invasion unfold on television. For most Americans, the invasion was a remote-control event, the type that you tune into occasionally to see if anything new has happened before turning the channel. The moral remove that Americans experienced as passive observers of a war being fought in their name coincided with, and was very likely caused by, the remove that American soldiers experienced from the battle itself. While many US soldiers fought and died in combat, a stunning number of them didn't, and this allowed the US citizenry to watch more comfortably from their armchairs. Like the ring of Gyges, the technological superiority of modern weaponry protected US forces from aggressive countermeasures. US soldiers used their own remote controls to direct one of the most devastating military assaults in the history of modern warfare. The technological superiority of the United States – its ability to strike with precision from a distance – produced the "shock and awe" relentlessly advertised by the media.

Of course, modern militaries want to achieve an advantage over their adversaries to make conflict as asymmetrical as possible. This, however, is a strategic determination (it is obviously better to defeat an opponent, strategically speaking), not a moral or a legal one (as there are certain tactics that militaries ought not to employ in the name of victory). In this chapter, we address the moral implications of the asymmetry that drones create on modern battlefields.[11] Similar concerns attend the use of manned aircraft that protect their pilots, but the rise of unmanned aerial systems encourages us to revisit and highlight certain dangers.

For a very long time, philosophers have assumed that warfare, unlike their own craft, cannot be conducted from an armchair. That may have been true in the past, but the rise of semiautonomous drones suggests that this assumption no longer obtains. Drone pilots now have what philosophers have always enjoyed, something Thomas Hobbes called "leisure," or freedom from constant threat of death. The "leisure" of drone pilots creates what Klem Ryan describes as "disassociation" between these soldiers and their violent acts. This is disturbing, according to Ryan, to the extent that this distance between pilots and their targets has clear "negative implications for compliance with the law." He cites a 2004 International Committee of the Red Cross report to this effect:

> Many studies have shown that people find it difficult to kill their fellow human beings at close range and that special conditioning is needed to overcome this inhibition. Conflicts in which recourse is had to advanced technologies which permit killing at a distance or on the computer screen prevent the activation of neuro-psychological mechanisms which render the act of killing difficult . . . The humanity of the other side is denied by attributing to the enemy contemptible character traits, intentions or behaviour: "We are superior, they are inferior." "We are fighting for an honourable and disinterested cause, they are fighting for inadmissible interests and objectives deserving only condemnation."[12]

If Ryan is right, and we think in general he is, the "leisure" that drone operators experience is a dangerous by-product of advanced military technologies.[13]

Yet, the leisure of drone pilots presents another possible implication. As Hobbes pointed out, those with leisure have the opportunity to think: "Leisure is the mother of philosophy."[14] Today, soldiers will have unprecedented opportunities to exercise reflection and moral judgment in their once-dangerous jobs. Whether troops seize these opportunities will depend on the will of military and political commanders but also on the initiative and ability of the pilots themselves. Drone technology shields soldiers from harm but also brings them closer to their targets – in the sense of close surveillance – than ever before. Ethics have long been taught to officer candidates and battlefield soldiers. But this new breed of remote-control soldier will have the time and the space to think through hitherto unseen moral quandaries, like the question of using a drone to kill an unarmed human being thousands of miles away or, in the case of signature strikes, the ability to kill at a distance on the basis of more vague behavior profiles. Similarly, the distance that drones create between the battlefield and citizens of aggressive nation-states *should* allow the leaders and their constituents to engage in ever more rigorous ethical and legal analyses concerning the status of military action. Whether this promise is fulfilled, however, remains to be seen.

Today, as drone technology shields soldiers and citizenry from the costs of war, they must face the disturbing prospect of having greater latitude in the strategic choices that they make and condone, even if these choices run counter to long-standing legal or ethical norms. Drone warfare makes fighting just wars easier (and this is unquestionably good), but it will also facilitate the prosecution of unjust wars. Additionally, our reliance on military robotics may tempt individuals to confuse just and unjust wars. This confusion is potentially unsettling to drone operators, and it should be. A 2011 Pentagon study, which anticipated the results of a detailed psychological study from 2012, showed that nearly 30 percent of drone pilots experience what the military calls "burnout," defined by the military as "an existential crisis."[15] As Robert Sparrow argues at length, the move to automate today's weaponry risks removing this human element of moral decision making, thereby removing the ethical responsibility that has traditionally constrained the way military actions are undertaken.[16] This may occur in the not-so-distant future, but for now human operators still have significant roles in most unmanned weapon systems. These individuals will continue to act on extremely vexing moral decisions, which result from difficult deliberations that stand in marked contrast to the easiness and expediency of drones' technical capabilities.

In the past, leaders and military strategists who initiated and oversaw military operations were supposed to shoulder the brunt of moral responsibility. This was appropriate since they did so from the relative safety of their fortified bunkers or, at the very least, from behind a row of protective ground troops. Commanders often had philosophical training to think through the complexities of their jobs. This type of training, we submit, helped commanders face the challenge of moral responsibility, even if it did not necessarily lead them to the right moral choice. To be clear, studying philosophy or ethics does not hardwire a student to be moral or to always do the right thing – again, automation is an attribute of robots, not humans – but it does give students practice in shouldering the responsibility of being a moral agent.

If soldiers have the tools to make informed moral decisions, then they should also be given the freedom to do so by creating greater legal space for selective conscientious objection or for disobeying orders on moral grounds.[17] Along these lines, Jeff McMahan has argued repeatedly that traditional just war theory should be reworked in several important ways.[18] He suggested that the tenets of a revised theory apply not only to governments, traditionally represented by commanders and heads of state, but also to individual soldiers. The justness of particular wars should be weighed by the consciences of individual war fighters. This is a significant revision since it broadens the scope of responsibility for warfare beyond political institutions to include the men and women who engage in combat. This has always been the case with the principles of *jus in bello* (the conventions or rules that govern military conduct) but McMahan intends individuals to be held responsible for the additional standards of *jus ad bellum*, those guidelines that describe the permissibility of initiating military operations.[19] Specifically, McMahan believes that individuals are to bear at least some responsibility for upholding "just cause" requirements. McMahan expects more of soldiers and, in this age of drones and leisure, he is right to do so.[20] He worries, we think rightly, that as drones become increasingly autonomous, the consciences of individual soldiers will no longer safeguard against the violation of just cause requirements. When wars are fought by machines and not people, who will ask the following questions: Why, exactly, are wars being fought in our name, and are these wars justified?

Technology and ethical reflection

There is a healthy chance that modern democracies will squander the opportunity to interrogate the justification of modern warfare and the legitimacy of drone warfare. While modern technology provides the leisure necessary for philosophical reflection, it tends to keep people otherwise occupied. This is, we believe, at the heart of the "disassociation" that Ryan so succinctly describes. Technological processes often run counter to the critical nature of philosophical inquiry and make ethical questions appear as unnecessary as they are difficult. Consequently, a philosophical lesson emerges: before one begins to memorize the specific tenets of international law, he or she must first grapple with the ethics of warfare. More specifically, one must acknowledge the radical extent to which modern technology has affected the way we think about warfare.

We are by no means the first to make this claim, but previous thinkers, from John Dewey to Herbert Marcuse and Martin Heidegger, did not write in the age of drones. Instead, they addressed the relationship between technology and warfare in a time defined by the mechanization of mass destruction (think trench warfare, Dresden, and Nagasaki). The widespread fear of total war and nuclear holocaust affected the uptake of these men's philosophical critiques of technology. The obvious nature of the problem, namely apocalyptic destruction, seemed perversely out of sync with the excruciating detail that defined their writings on technology. No one needed a very smart philosopher to explain the dangers of an arms race. At most, they needed the British philosopher, Bertrand Russell, to articulate general intuitions into philosophical arguments (as he did in *Common Sense and Nuclear Warfare*).[21] The risk of combat drones is not nearly as obvious or as widespread (at least not yet) and so philosophers must present more nuanced arguments for drone regulation. Drone warfare suggests that the dangers of technology can be subtler, pernicious in their subtlety, and that these dangers cannot be negotiated away through prudential reasoning (the sort of reasoning that turns on an evaluation of self-interest). Cost-benefit analyses alone cannot limit the use of drones or precision-guided munitions, as they did with nuclear armaments, precisely because these new technologies are meant to mitigate costs. These weapons, as opposed to techniques of mass destruction, are heralded as precise, smart, and just.

Today, we need a more nuanced philosophical analysis, like that of Marcuse, to get to the heart of the problem and to critique a system that typifies "technological rationality."[22] In 1941, Marcuse argued that Nazi Germany reflected the type of rationality that subordinates human autonomy to the direction of machines. To be clear, we are not suggesting that our rising drone culture is the same as Nazi Germany (it is not), but we are suggesting that they may share a common attitude toward military mechanization. Marcuse was ahead of his time, though perfectly suited to ours. He writes that "the decisive point is that this attitude – which dissolves all actions into a sequence of semi-spontaneous reactions to pre-scribed mechanical norms – is not only perfectly rational but also perfectly reasonable."[23]

By "reasonable," Marcuse means that the use of certain technologies – in this case drones, precision-guided muni-tions, and satellite uplinks – has become commonplace in our modern military-industrial complex. Targeted killings will be conducted with the help of drones, even in relatively peaceful times from now on. Marcuse suggests that it is always uncom-fortable to object to the commonplace and the unspoken. The normalization of certain technological processes, he main-tains, renders "all protest senseless, and the individual who would insist on his freedom of action would become a crank." Only cranks would protest the use of weapons that promise to limit collateral damage. Only cranks would point out that this promise makes their use more likely, if not inevitable. Marcuse suggests that "there is no personal escape [for these cranks or anyone else] from the apparatus which has mecha-nized and standardized the world. It is a rational apparatus, combining utmost expediency with utmost convenience, saving time and energy, removing waste, adapting all means to the end, anticipating consequences, sustaining calculability and security."

Expediency, convenience, calculability, security – this sums up the US drone program between 2003 and 2013 quite nicely. But future soldiers and the rest of the US population now have the time to attend to other descriptors that are antithetical to technological rationality: morality, reflection, deliberation, and autonomy. Morality is not expedient. Careful reflection takes too long and too much effort to be convenient (it is usually quite hard); deliberation comes from the verb "to weigh" (as in the scales of justice), not the verb "to compute" (as in to make a calculation); and autonomy is more about maintaining freedom than it is about security. One serious moral problem with the age of drones is that modern democracies risk forgetting, and in some cases purposely obscure, these important distinctions. It is tempting to think that ease and convenience are virtues, but it is best to resist this temptation because they have never been and never will be.[24]

Marcuse suspected his argument would come as a shock at a moment when saving time and energy are paramount values and when "being easy" is often interchangeable with "being good." But here we echo Marcuse: let us be shocked. Think of all the things that are easy to do and are morally questionable – it is easy to exploit the powerless, easy to abuse a child, easy to lie to the gullible, easy to litter, easy to fixate on material wealth, easy to be sexist, easy to cause animal suffering, easy to ignore the hungry. From a military standpoint, it is easy also for certain countries to kill people with Hellfire missiles. Some of the easiest things in life are some of the most immoral, and that is why *all* of the easiest things are, or should be, morally suspect. Suspicion will not always lead to judgments of guilt, but the ease of a particular activity should place our ethical sensibilities on high alert.

While particular decisions by the Obama Administration to conduct signature strikes may have been difficult, the technical precision of military devices made once-impossible

decisions substantially easier – easy enough that such decisions became routinized and drew little public attention.
Citizens and armchair soldiers, who watch and wage wars
from the comfort of their homes, should be on the lookout for
moral hazards and what Hannah Arendt termed the "banality
of evil." The next section unpacks this concept in reference
to the rise of drone warfare and temporarily shifts the discussion from the responsibility of nation-states and war fighters
to the often-overlooked responsibility of citizens who tacitly
support potentially problematic policies. Arendt coined the
term "banality of evil" in her analysis of the Nazi regime, but
her interest was not with unjust acts so much as the mentality
that often gives rise to them. It is this mentality that we must
attune ourselves to in the age of semiautonomous weaponry.
Nevertheless, it is extremely important to recognize that we
are not suggesting that drone strikes are comparable to the
Holocaust. In legal and moral terms, these acts are very, very
different.

The "banality of evil" revisited: the case of drones[25]

World War II is often a reference point for discussion about
the moral problem of evil in warfare, but what we stand to
learn from this history may come as a surprise. When Arendt
looked back, she learned that Holocaust-grade evil is not the
product of exceptionally wicked people, but rather surprisingly
ordinary ones behaving unusually thoughtlessly. Therein lies
the "banality of evil." Since 2001, the United States has fought
and fetishized a form of radical evil. In so doing, its citizens
may have lost sight of the fact that there is another, banal kind
of evil: the moral dangers associated with drones and other
semiautonomous military technologies. Many public statements by the current administration, including President

Obama's 2009 Nobel Peace Prize speech, demonstrate confusion between these two varieties of evil. In Oslo, the president averred: "Evil does exist in the world. A non-violent movement could not have halted Hitler's armies. Negotiations cannot convince Al-Qaeda's leaders to lay down their arms. To say that force may sometimes be necessary is not a call to cynicism – it is a recognition of history, the imperfections of man and the limits of reason."[26] Al-Qaeda, however, is not tantamount to Hitler and his followers – a fact that becomes clear when we rethink the banality of evil. To explore drone warfare in terms of the banality of evil is potentially disturbing for many readers, but it is the type of food for thought that is best consumed before, and to avoid the emergence of, morally problematic situations.

Arendt was a reporter for the *New Yorker* at the trial of Adolf Eichmann in April 1961. Eichmann was a lieutenant colonel in the Nazi SS and one of the masterminds of the Holocaust. Arendt, like most people, probably expected Eichmann to be a monster, some anti-Semitic zealot who took singular pleasure in the persecution of the Jews. Surprisingly, he did not live up to these expectations. Arendt wrote: "The trouble with Eichmann was precisely that so many were like him, and that the many were neither perverted nor sadistic, that they were, and still are, terribly and terrifyingly normal. From the viewpoint of our legal institutions and of our moral standards of judgment, this normality was much more terrifying than all the atrocities put together." What was terrifying about Eichmann was that someone so boring could commit such extraordinarily evil acts. He had no unique commitment to a radical ideology, no special loyalty to a fiendish leader, no *sui generis* desire to torture or kill. He was just doing his job. Arendt's point concerning the banality of evil was also taken up by Milton Mayer in his description of Weimar Germany in *They Thought They Were Free*. Mayer explains that the

Holocaust was brought on by "the gradual habituation of the people, little by little, to being governed by surprise; to receiving decisions deliberated in secret."[27] This habituation – one that could easily describe the unawareness of the US public vis-à-vis drone warfare – occurred in such a way that the people believed, in Mayer's words, "that the situation was so complicated that the government had to act on information which the people could not understand, or so dangerous that, even if the people could not understand it, it could not be released because of national security."[28]

Such deference on matters of national security describes the general ethos surrounding US drone strikes quite nicely: the Obama Administration has to act in response to an exceptionally complex geopolitical situation defined by unprecedented dangers. Exceptional threats from non-state actors warrant the enlargement of government (and especially executive) powers. As Mayer explains, this enlargement of governmental powers often occurs at a distance from public consensus:

> This separation of government from people, this widening of the gap, took place so gradually and so insensibly, each step disguised (perhaps not even intentionally) as a temporary emergency measure or associated with true patriotic allegiance or with real social purposes. And all the crises and reforms (real reforms, too) so occupied the people that they did not see the slow motion underneath, of the whole process of government growing remoter and remoter.[29]

Arendt, however, maintains that this distance between onlookers and active participants does not free onlookers from responsibility. Indeed, for Arendt, the opposite is the case: crimes that reflect the banality of evil are usually "committed en masse, not only in regard to the number of victims, but also in regard to the numbers of those who perpetrated the crime, and the extent to which any one of the many criminals was close to or remote from the actual killer of the victim means nothing, as far as the measure of his responsibility is concerned." This statement implies that onlookers or individuals who play supporting roles in morally questionable acts should also be held responsible. In a radical claim, Arendt puts the matter thus: "in general *the degree of responsibility increases as we draw further away from the man who uses the fatal instrument with his own hands*" (emphasis added).[30]

In the case of the ethics of drone warfare, the implication of Arendt's claim is somewhat counterintuitive: those who are most responsible may not be the men and women who operate combat drones but rather the stunningly large supporting cast that tacitly or explicitly endorses these strikes – from the government to the public at large. The admission that average people *like us* could be responsible for, or complicit in, unjust acts of varying scale and severity is the truly gut-wrenching aspect of the Eichmann trial. According to Arendt, the case stood as a painful reminder that evil could be born in the midst of the commonplace, in an age and a culture that operated seamlessly, precisely, unstoppably, to obscure the injustices it committed. This point applies directly to the Third Reich, but also serves as a necessary warning to any well-ordered society. Arendt suggested that the horror of the Holocaust was a product of ordinary people like Eichmann thoughtlessly going through the motions of a well-ordered, yet morally flawed, society. The banality of evil emerges in the tyranny of the thoughtless majority. This is what Arendt meant when she suggested "There is a strange interdependence between thoughtlessness and evil."[31]

Herein lies the difference between the evil of the Holocaust and that of Islamic extremism. Islamic extremism is, by definition, radical. There is nothing banal about it. Islamic extremism requires significant sacrifices from individuals, who use violence or the threat of it to compel an otherwise unwilling group to accede to a set of demands. These terroristic or guerrilla tactics, undertaken by enthusiastic volunteers, are employed around the world. The attacks of September 11, 2001, comprise part of a global insurgency with strategic principles that underpinned much of the subsequent insurgent action in Afghanistan and Iraq. Whatever one may think of the Islamic extremists' "cause," they usually use *radical transgression of societal norms as a means* through which they can achieve their objectives. These objectives are not always clear but they have included: expelling the United States from Saudi Arabia; restoring the Islamic caliphate; establishing an Islamic state; forcing a national government to withdraw from a war; and so on. The radical nature of violent Islamic extremism makes it very different from Eichmann's case.

For Eichmann and his fellow Nazis, their radical views came to pervade social norms to such an extent that their actions did not seem extreme in context. The total dehumanization of the Jewish people by the National Socialist regime, together with threats of retribution to deter any type of assistance to Jews and the bureaucratization of systematic extermination, created a unique set of self-reinforcing societal norms. It became easy for individuals, such as Eichmann – and much of the German population – to acquiesce to the total marginalization, and attempted extermination, of the Jewish community. In fact, it was much easier for Germans to accept Nazi policies than to oppose them. Eichmann's actions thus conformed to the normative and legal imperatives of his society. In contrast to banality, then, the radicalism of evil emerges in an obsessive, highly motivated minority, rather than from within a conditioned thoughtless majority. Of course, we acknowledge that Islamic extremists also undergo conditioning and operate within their own distinct "society" – but most have made a decision to join that other society, having been previously immersed in one that prohibits extralegal acts of terrorism.

The trial of Adolf Eichmann carries an implicit warning to liberal democracies like the United States: beware the normalization of the extraordinary. The Nazis did not suddenly seize power and implement the Final Solution, they did so slowly and incrementally. While current drone policies are not harbingers of an Orwellian state or the systematic extermination of populations abroad, caution is certainly warranted. Each step toward Nazi dominance was a step toward a state that normalized extraordinarily unjust policies – the permanent "state of exception," as Giorgio Agamben termed it, whereby the previously unthinkable becomes accepted as normal.[32] Critics frequently point out that the indefinite detention of "enemy combatants" represents just such a situation. But what about the expanded use of drones and the revelation that President Obama personally oversees a "kill list"? And what about White House Press Secretary Jay Carney's recent assertion that the use of drones is "legal, ethical, and wise"? Are we to take Carney at his word and happily accept this unusual statement as a description of a brave new world? The authors of this volume would prefer not to.

The United States outlawed assassination in 1976, following the revelation that the CIA had attempted to kill various foreign leaders, including Fidel Castro. The Obama Administration's justification for its revival of assassination as a tool of foreign policy rests upon the same rationale as President George W. Bush's: since the United States is "at war" with al-Qaeda, it is not a violation of the ban against peacetime assassination. Whereas Bush made this argument about the invasion of Iraq, Obama made the same claim about "targeted killings." The Bush Administration also initiated extant drone policies; though, as discussed in chapter 2, the practice has expanded substantially under President Obama. The American public seems largely uninterested in engaging with the moral and legal issues raised by drones; their use is accepted as militarily necessary. Ironically, Obama's policy of targeted killings may be more popular with the

American public *because* it does away with the stubborn problem presented by the indefinite detention of terrorist suspects. According to public opinion polls discussed earlier, a majority of Americans approve of drones' continued use abroad. To use Arendt's words, drone strikes in the last decade became "terribly and terrifyingly normal."

Technological rationality and its impact on just war theory

Although theories of technological rationality developed in a nonmilitary context, they have important bearing on ongoing discussions of just war theory and its application to international law. Indeed, today's international legal theorist must approach challenging IHL questions with a perspective informed by an understanding of how human attitudes toward military technologies influence normative frameworks. Unfortunately, insights from ethical theory and the philosophy of technology are often overlooked in treatments of drone warfare. We believe they should not be. The "technological rationality," described in our treatment of Marcuse above, for example, may answer the questions that have long troubled philosophers concerned with the ethics of war and peace. Our faith in technological capabilities may make asking questions about the long-standing tenets of distinction and proportionality seem unnecessarily difficult, or more starkly, simply unnecessary. It is the responsibility of ethicists, however, to ask these questions. A growing number of ethicists have turned their attention to the ethics of drones. In some cases, these ethicists have argued for the legitimacy of drones, and indeed argued that the use of these technologies is morally obligatory. We will turn attention to this argument for a moment to access the strengths and weaknesses of the claim, concluding that drones remain morally problematic despite their precision.

Drones as morally obligatory?

Some philosophers, such as Bradley Strawser, have argued that drones' greater efficacy – as compared with prior, less precise technologies – makes their use morally obligatory. This contention is problematic, however, because it places too much emphasis on the relationship between commander and soldier, and insufficient emphasis on the larger moral context in which both commander and soldier operate. Here we challenge Strawser's general claim, not only as a matter of philosophical debate, but also because we fear that the policy community increasingly shares his views.

In 2010, Strawser provided a philosophical argument supporting drone use, and argues that, all things being equal, unmanned aerial vehicles make fighting just wars safer and more likely and therefore their use is morally obligatory. This is formulated in the following manner: "For any just action taken by a given military, if it is possible for the military to use UAV platforms in place of inhabited aerial vehicles without a significant loss of capability, then that military has an ethical obligation to do so."[33] Strawser draws this conclusion on the basis of what he terms the principle of unnecessary risk (PUR). PUR is given to Strawser's reader in the following way:

> PUR proceeds as follows: If X gives Y an order to accomplish good goal G, then X has an obligation, other things being equal, to cho[o]se a means to accomplish G that does not violate the demands of justice, make the world worse, or expose Y to potentially lethal risk unless incurring such risk aids in the accomplishment of G in some way that cannot be gained via less risky means. That is, it is wrong to command someone to take on *unnecessary* potentially lethal risks in an effort to carry out a just action for some good; any potentially lethal risk incurred must be justified by some strong countervailing reason. In the absence of such a reason, ordering someone to incur potentially lethal risk is morally impermissible. Importantly, PUR is a demand not to order someone to take

> unnecessary risk *on par* with alternative means to accomplish some goal G. This is what the other things being equal clause is meant to capture. That is, in some cases, the only possible way to accomplish G will be to order Y to undertake a particular means which exposes Y to potentially lethal risk. In such cases, PUR is not directly applicable; whether or not the order is justified must be determined on other grounds. PUR simply demands that no *more* risk than is required for the accomplishment of G . . . is ordered by X to be incurred by Y.[34]

The stipulation that introduces PUR, namely that a military is pursuing a good goal G and not violating demands of justice, is crucially important for Strawser's argument, which focuses on the use of drones *in principle*. This stipulation, while circumscribing the argument to the principled use of drones, significantly constrains the explanatory and normative force of his analysis of drones. This is a point that Uwe Steinhoff develops at length. Strawser suggests that PUR is uncontroversial, but Steinhoff rightly states that this is only "because there are so many provisos already built into it."[35]

The stakes for Strawser's argument are not merely academic – we are concerned that many policy makers share his view that using drones to minimize risks to soldiers is morally obligatory. For the imperative to use drones to obtain, however, one must accept several premises, which are very difficult to establish. The primary premise is "that choosing UAVs to obtain a military goal does not violate the demands of justice . . . that it does not make the world worse off; and that it does not expose Y to potentially lethal risk."[36] Strawser recognizes this, but does not seem to regard it as jeopardizing his philosophical argument. He states: "The justification of remotely controlled weapons in war here assumes that their employment is done as part of a fully justified war effort meeting both *jus ad bellum* and *jus in bello* criteria." This is an assumption that is safe to make in principle, but definitely not in practice. Strawser often recognizes this fact, but policy makers and citizens may not. Indeed, as Steinhoff observes, there is a significant difference between PUR and Strawser's conclusion at other points, namely that he often does not include the stipulations of PUR. Steinhoff reads Strawser charitably and assumes that most of Strawser's conclusions about the obligatory nature of drone use actually imply the provisos of PUR, but we think that the broad-stroke conclusion concerning the imperative to use combat drones *without the provisos* may be the conclusion that some policy makers accept in the drone age.

Our primary concern in this chapter is that the expanded use of drones may allow soldiers, leaders, and their constituents to circumvent the hard questions concerning the laws of war and the justification of modern warfare in liberal democracies. Strawser's argument, for the most part, avoids this issue. Along these lines, Rebecca Johnson writes that "[c]oncerns that the existence of unmanned systems hastens decision makers down a slippery slope toward targeting civilians for acts of complicity both ignores the widespread use of similar practices throughout history and ignores the very real scrutiny both personality and signature strikes receive before they are authorized."[37] In general, we agree with some of Strawser's narrower conclusions. For instance: "If the military in question is justified in a particular military strike in the first place, they should protect the just warrior carrying out the action to the greatest extent as is possible up until protecting the warrior impedes his/her ability to behave justly in combat."[38] Michael Walzer and others, however, have argued that making modern war fighters unsusceptible to harm may in fact impede one in behaving justly in combat or in making just decisions about going to war in the first place (as the myth of Gyges so pointedly demonstrates).[39] Following Susy

Killmister, Jacoby Carter has also argued that the radical difference between the drone pilot (and other modern military personnel) and most enemy combatants creates a situation in which enemy combatants (unable to protect themselves by traditional, moral military means) might be morally justified in resorting to other tactics of asymmetric warfare when faced with potential drone strikes.[40]

A final objection to Strawser's argument resonates closely with the central thrust of the politics chapter of this volume – that the essential function of weaponized drones are geared toward those covert military activities that increasingly define counter-insurgency, and that those activities undermine the ways that modern democracies have determined the legitimacy of military activity. Steven Levine, in his critique of Strawser, suggests that this essential fit between drones and covert operations risks undercutting democratic accountability.[41] Much like the use of poison, drones are meant to kill quickly and surreptitiously. Levine notes that the military tactics fitted to drones are surreptitious so as to catch targets unaware, but they are not the only ones left in the dark about these targeted strikes. The citizens that support militaries with drone capabilities also remain unaware of the prevalence or nature of drone strikes (a fact that cannot simply be attributed to willing ignorance). This proves to be a very fruitful line of critique against Strawser's argument. Levine writes:

> In lowering the cost of use, drones do not just make war too tempting, they also make assassinations and secret intelligence operations too tempting. Drones and their *specific capabilities*, i.e., their accuracy and ability to be guided in real-time with no threat to their operator, make them uniquely suited to these types of operations. For in reducing collateral damage and the risk of the mission overall, they lower the visibility of the operation and the potential for pushback not

just by those attacked but by other actors, i.e., domestic constituencies concerned about the mission, other governments, international bodies and NGOs, etc. Strawser bemoans the secret nature of the drone program, and argues that a just program needs a transparent legal framework. What he does not consider is the possibility that secrecy is not a contingent feature of US drone policy, but is endemic to the technology and its *likely*, i.e., not ideal, use.[42]

Levine's analysis coincides closely with the concerns that we raised in chapter 3 and has important implications for the way we conceive of the proper relationship between liberal democratic governments and their citizens, but more broadly, between liberal ideals and security.

Collateral damage – blurring the fact–value distinction[43]

One of the things that could prevent a clear-eyed assessment of international law and just war theory in reference to the use of drones in targeted killings is the enduring confusion – which is symptomatic of technological rationality – between facts and values. Strawser and others have argued that drones allow modern military personnel to distinguish more carefully between licit and illicit targets, therefore upholding the principle of distinction that was discussed in the earlier chapter on the legal implications of drones. This may be true in many cases, but a potential confusion concerning distinction needs to be discussed. This confusion is reflected in each of the preceding sections. The myth of Gyges strikes a reader as morally objectionable because Gyges confuses what is expedient with what is just. More pointedly, given that the act is expedient, Gyges does not consider whether it is just. Marcuse is concerned about the same conflation in his critique of technology, and Arendt believed that the banality of evil could take hold in well-ordered societies that understand order as necessarily good ("order" being a matter of fact, while "goodness" being a matter of value).

It may seem strange to underscore and maintain this distinction between facts and values because of the obviousness of the observation that facts are always already value-laden.[44] It is not possible to make a factual statement without belying a certain normative framework; the philosopher Hilary Putnam states, quite rightly, that facts always come to us "screaming with values."[45] And as pragmatists, we believe that values arise in the thick of things and do not exist in some otherworldly place devoid of facts. That being said, on many occasions, there is an important distinction to be made between statements of fact and statements of value. (Putnam, despite his attempt to collapse the fact–value distinction, agrees with us on this point.) Additionally, readers will never find a case in which they can deduce moral prescriptions, in any straightforward way, from a set of exclusively empirical descriptions. Empirical observations can certainly play a role, even a very large one, in our moral determinations, but we tend to agree with David Hume that at the end of the day an "ought" cannot be derived from an "is." This point is lost on many proponents of US drone policy. It is therefore worth restating it and explaining how losing sight of it may impact interpretations of the ethical and legal implications of drone warfare.

Let us begin with a statement of fact: "Unmanned aerial vehicles and precision-guided munitions usually allow modern militaries to destroy object X without destroying nearby object Y." This is an accurate description of technical capabilities. In the coming century, modern militaries will increase their precision in targeting certain objects while sparing others. This fact, however, does not deliver us seamlessly to the conclusion that "Unmanned aerial vehicles and precision-guided munitions allow modern militaries to target militants while sparing non-combatants."[46] Why not? The distinction between militants and non-combatants, between licit and illicit targets, is a normative one that machines cannot make – now or in some brave new world. It is not just an issue of destroying one object and not destroying another. We are sure this comes as a disappointment to many, but as asymmetric conflict and guerilla warfare increase in frequency and intensity (and we think there is every reason to suspect they will), the moral and legal distinctions between licit and illicit targets will become harder, not easier, to make. As we argue in the following section, it is in no way clear that new drones and munitions will help cut through the fog of war that will undoubtedly thicken in coming years.

We suggest that a tension emerges in the discourse surrounding drones. Drones will only get better and more efficient in terms of their technical capabilities. However, the legal and ethical questions will remain vexed. It would be convenient to think that technical capabilities could fill in for the moral judgment of humans, but it would also be profoundly wrong. A reader may think that this error is so obvious that no one would be tempted to make it. This confusion, however, is reflected in numerous comments – official and unofficial – concerning surgical military strikes after the invasion of Iraq. In a 2003 press conference, then Secretary of Defense Donald Rumsfeld stated: "Our military capabilities are so devastating and precise that we can destroy an Iraqi tank under a bridge without damaging the bridge. We do not need to kill thousands of innocent Iraqis to remove Saddam Hussein from power. At least that's our belief. We believe we can destroy his institutions of power and oppression in an orderly manner."[47]

In this case, Rumsfeld slips from touting the technical capabilities of the US military to describing the normative or legal distinctions concerning the ability to spare innocents while aiming at legitimate targets. Today, the international community faces an inevitability that Walzer described three decades ago: the point at which the ends of military campaigns are fit, with stunning precision, to the technical capabilities at our disposal, a point where only the considerations of justice itself stand to set limits on these ends. As our technological precision increases, the specificity and exactitude of our moral decisions must keep pace.

Conclusion

This chapter engaged a few key issues in the ethics of drone warfare and addressed a select number of the philosophical positions on the subject. It opened with the moral hazard associated with the use of armed drones. In coming decades, given that non-state actors will continue to pose a threat to national security, modern militaries will pursue technologies that are engineered to target and monitor these threats. This is undoubtedly judicious, but doing so comes with the ability to conduct military operations at ever lower costs and this presents a moral hazard – a situation where an actor takes on risky behavior while not shouldering the consequences or risks of said behavior. The highly automated nature of tomorrow's warfare will place soldiers who operate these weapon systems in a position to squarely confront this moral hazard with unprecedented clarity. They should be trained not only technically but also morally and legally to grapple with this issue. This normative reckoning will be difficult but essential to prevent targeted killings by drones from becoming banal. It is only by problematizing the assumptions underlying US drone policies that citizens and decision makers can grapple with the manifold implications of this new technology of warfare. In particular, this process of deliberation and critique will empower citizens to make value-based judgments about the use of drones – which, we hope, will inform policy debates and increase the democratic accountability of decision makers overseeing the drone program.

As we stated in the chapter on politics, it is likely that widespread policy reform will take place only if citizens and decision makers realize that the use of drones in military strikes actually stands to compromise US interests or the values of its citizenry. At the end of the day, prudential, rather than moral, reasoning often holds sway in deliberations about warfare. We are aware of this and, in the conclusion to this book, we attempt to give several prudential arguments against overreliance on unmanned aerial weapon systems. Additionally, in the conclusion, we propose a number of policy recommendations to regulate the continued use of drones.

CHAPTER SIX

Conclusion: The Way Ahead

"Before the war, the Predator had skeptics, because it did not fit the old ways. Now it is clear the military does not have enough unmanned vehicles. We're entering an era in which unmanned vehicles of all kinds will take on greater importance."

Former President George W. Bush, 2001[1]

Unmanned aerial vehicles have offered great promise for the countries that fly them or those that hope to acquire them. The United States has not just increased the frequency of drone strikes but also expanded the geographic location, lured by the low-risk prospects and tactical utility. While the reliance on drones raises questions of strategic effectiveness – whether the strikes cause more terrorists than they kill – the domestic political environment has made the use of drones an appealing option in the counterterrorism toolkit. The concluding chapter begins by reviewing those political arguments. It turns to the international legal implications that were discussed in chapter 4. It then revisits the moral implications outlined in chapter 5.

The majority of the arguments presented in this book have focused on the current use of drones by the United States in asymmetric conflict. This conclusion, however, turns to broader questions, especially about the future. What happens after the countries that are acquiring combat drones have done so? What does the long-term picture of drone use look like? What are the actual rules of the road or the norms guiding the use of drones and the institutional vehicle through which these norms operate? What institutional arrangements are suited to the question of drone proliferation?

To this end, we suggest that there are instrumental reasons for the United States to limit the way it uses drones, to be even more transparent in terms of the conditions in which it conducts its strikes, and to take a lead role in the international regime that helps regulate the use of drones. First, while drones are tactically effective, their strategic effectiveness is limited. Drones may kill terrorists with ruthless efficiency, but they leave the fundamental drivers behind terrorism unaddressed – and they may even exacerbate those motivations. Second, by limiting its current use, the United States can help set the grounds for limiting how others use drones in the future. In other words, more self-constraints in the short term can create the conditions for constraining others' use in the future, with important implications for regional and international stability. Third, except in certain narrow cases, preferable alternatives to drones exist. Placing American boots on the ground may not only be more moral and legal, but – as the US army's COIN manual suggests – it is also likely more effective over the long term. However, we also acknowledge the important role that certain military technologies, including robotics, may play in protecting US troops in combat as well as supporting them with the best intelligence.

Thus, even if readers are unconvinced by the legal and ethical reasons to be wary of drones, then perhaps these instrumental reasons should be considered. This chapter considers the prudential basis for carefully considering the extent of drone use. Thus, after reviewing the main themes of the book and revisiting the question of proliferation, we turn to these questions about the prudential use of drones.

The politics of drones

As we discussed in chapter 3, the use of drones offers a number of political advantages. Most importantly, they do not risk American casualties. A number of scholars have found that, as casualties rise, opposition to conflict also rises; to the extent that public consent is required to initiate and continue military operations, then opposition constrains leaders' strategic options.[2] Thus, the appeal of drones is that they do not introduce casualties, which means that their use can minimize decision-making constraints. Fewer constraints, however, are mixed blessings to the extent that the latitude that drone technologies gives policy makers may encourage them to engage in far-ranging military objectives without the consent of their constituents, thus presenting the problem of democratic accountability outlined in chapter three. An analysis published by the UK Ministry of Defence put this problem in the form of a question:

> Will decision-makers resort to war as a policy option far sooner than previously? Clausewitz himself suggests that it is policy that prevents the escalation of the brutality of war to its absolute form via a diabolical escalatory feedback loop – one of the contributory factors in controlling and limiting aggressive policy is the risk to one's own forces. It is essential that, before unmanned systems become ubiquitous (if it is not already too late) . . . we consider this issue and ensure that, by removing some of the horror, or at least keeping it at a distance, . . . we do not risk losing our controlling humanity and make war more likely.[3]

Perhaps supporting the concerns underlying this danger, combat drones triggered minimal scrutiny and opposition in the United States in the first several years of their use, granting leaders enormous latitude in how they carried out the policy. Even in more recent years, a strong majority of

Americans have supported the use of drones to target suspected militants. Indeed, the public's enthusiasm for drones has become part of the political discourse on drones. These top-line figures of support, however, result in part because polls themselves are contributing to the marketplace of ideas through the assumptions embedded in the polls. Polls are silent on the question of authorization, despite criticisms that have arisen about whether drone strikes are authorized under domestic or international law. Additionally, polls incorporate the debatable assertion that drone strikes target high-level militants or terrorists.

In contrast to the American public's apparent support, international audiences are not particularly enamored with drones. The Pakistani public has increasingly opposed the use of drones and the Pakistani prime minister elected on May 11, 2013, Nawaz Sharif, has told his cabinet that "the policy of protesting against drone strikes for public consumption, while working behind the scenes to make them happen, is not on."[4] His subsequent speech to the UN General Assembly further suggested dissatisfaction with drones, although the speeches may simply be domestic political theater, as a number of sources have suggested that privately and tacitly Pakistan has given its consent for the strikes.[5] Nonetheless, all politics is local and, to the extent that the American public is more preoccupied with the targeting of *Americans*, the use of drones abroad will remain attractive politically and democratic accountability will remain inoperative.

In chapter 3, we also argued that neither the legislative nor judicial branch has offered meaningful constraints on the executive's reach and autonomy on drone strikes. While some legal analysts have suggested the establishment of oversight panels such as the FISA court system, we are not persuaded that this is an effective means of self-regulation, especially in light of revelations that the FISA court has not only not constrained leaders but actually expanded their reach. Instead, we suggest that the more fruitful forms of restraint would come from Congress. In particular, we would encourage the executive to follow through on a suggestion made in May 2013 that the United States consider terminating the Authorization for Use of Military Force (AUMF) and the adjustments that were made to this document in the 2012 National Defense Authorization Act. More than a decade after the 9/11 attacks, the almost entirely unfettered capacity of executive authority to use military force seems unwarranted. On a number of occasions, President Obama has fallen back on the AUMF to justify actions domestically that are at odds with the United States' commitments internationally, particularly on where the United States can conduct "self-defense" operations with the use of drones. The blanket authorization offered under the AUMF has contributed to executive power that Congress and the judiciary have had little success in keeping in check.

International law and drones

The chapter on international law suggested that, while the government has defended the use of drones as consistent with international legal commitments, there are reasons to be dubious. First, the self-defense justification, *jus ad bellum*, is based on an unclear operationalization of "imminence," which makes it difficult to assess compatibility with the requirement that a threat be "instant, overwhelming, and leaving no choice of means, and no moment of deliberation."[6] That said, a number of scholars have questioned whether many of the individuals targeted qualify even under a liberal definition of imminence, as many are low-level members of al-Qaeda who do not appear to have been planning an attack.

The case for adhering to *jus in bello* is no less murky. The central problem is that the principles of distinction and proportionality are fraught with problems of interpretation. In contemporary warfare, distinguishing between civilians and combatants is highly problematic, with individuals going back and forth between involvement in hostilities and civilian "bystanding," creating a "revolving door" between combatant and civilian. In addition, the question of proportionality is not necessarily adjudicated by a simple calculation of the number of civilians per total fatalities. Our central critique on *jus in bello* is that leaders have pointed to technology and precision as answering the call for distinction when technology and automation cannot judge the subtle distinction between civilian and combatant, or what level of military gain is necessary to be considered proportionate. These are questions that legal experts and courts have wrestled with and cannot adequately be addressed by an algorithm. Thus, while we acknowledge that, as a technology, precision munitions and drones are more humane than fire-bombing entire cities, we suggest that states should not be under the illusion that technology is solving subjective decisions about combatant status that are complex under the best of circumstances.

There are efforts that the hegemonic country – in this case the United States – can make to create a stable international order regarding the use of drones. The first step is domestic action – in concert with international actors – to articulate clearly and transparently how US policies conform with international law. To date, these arguments have been vague and therefore take on a certain arbitrariness that will create an unwieldy precedent for future use. Consequently, the United States should conduct hearings on the use of drones, evaluating the political and legal implications of their use. These meetings should not be conducted in isolation from the international community or broader discussions of IHL. We share Zenko's hope that such discussions will set the stage for a detailed explanation "of which legal principles apply – and do not apply – to drone strikes and the procedural safeguards to ensure compliance to build broader international consensus."[7]

Along these lines, we suggest that further measures be taken to examine the targeting practices themselves. This is not simply an issue of counting the number of people killed in a given attack, but rather entails a detailed legal discussion (informed by the philosophy of law). Such a discussion would address the following points:

- the definition of what constitutes collateral damage (as we saw in the discussion of ethics this is no easy determination to make);
- the use of the doctrine of double-effect (the position that holds that the intention behind a particular military action rather than the consequences of such an action forms the basis for the justification of a military strike);
- the concept of imminent threat in general and specifically in an age of weapons of mass destruction;
- the relationship between realistic threat assessment and proportionality, including acknowledgement of the high possibility of terrorist attacks of various scale on the US homeland;
- the concept of distinction – who is a combatant and who is not – in the age of asymmetric warfare;
- the relationship between intelligence gathering, surgical strikes, and detention practices.

In addition to being more judicious with its own use of drones, the United States could also take the lead internationally. As we suggest in the last sections of this chapter, how the United States approaches these questions in public forums will help establish the precedent and understanding of customary law on which other countries base their future targeting decisions.

The moral hazards of drones

In addressing the ethical challenges that drone warfare presents, we have explained the way that the use of drone technology could present a moral hazard for current and emerging drone powers. Drones limit the costs of war, both in blood and treasure, and therefore create a tempting situation for militaries and governments that have them at their disposal. They are tempted to engage in morally or legally questionable activities now that semiautonomous and precision technologies help them avoid the consequences that had always attended these actions. In an interesting tension, technologies such as drones may create a moral hazard, but also create the leisure for soldiers and their commanders to reflect on the intricacies of military ethics in unprecedentedly careful ways, that is, of course, if they can resist the temptation of moral hazards. We explore some of these avenues for further reflection.

Drones demonstrate how assumptions about technology and expediency can radically alter collective understanding of warfare and its justification. We regard this as the necessary background to understand the challenge that drone strikes pose to traditional just war theory and traditional military ethics. In the fourth chapter, we provided a brief survey of the apposite literature on the ethics of drones, focusing on the arguments presented by Bradley J. Strawser, and then concluded with a number of points concerning the principle of distinction and proportionality. With regard to distinction, there are ambiguities of targeting practices in asymmetric warfare (present in any weapon system) but drones present a particular risk that technical precision (an issue of fact) will be confused with moral or legal precision (an issue of value). Similarly, as Walzer points out in the context of proportionality, the means and tactics of war fighting can shape the particular ends that militaries pursue.

As detailed in chapter 5, the discussion of drone warfare has only recently turned to its moral implications. Robert Sparrow and Bradley Strawser were among the first to initiate this move, but only a handful of policy recommendations have emerged from their philosophical analyses. In a report otherwise focused on political and legal dimensions, Zenko makes a recommendation with important moral implications. He writes that current and emerging drone powers should "never conduct non-battlefield targeted killings without an accountable human being authorizing the strike." He goes on to stipulate that this does not rule out the possibility of autonomous drones using lethal force *in warfare*, in particular circumstances. While we agree with him on this first point, one that is often overlooked in the discussions of drone warfare, we are very hesitant to follow Zenko on the subsequent stipulation.

When it comes to lethal force, there should always be a human who is responsible for executing it. To date, drones remain remotely piloted, rather than fully autonomous, meaning that individuals trained in the law of armed conflict are still responsible for flying and targeting. Military centers such as the United States Naval Academy's Stockdale Center for Ethical Leadership, for example, should organize additional ethical and moral training – it already does a great deal of work along these lines – that goes beyond the standard training. While this training should center on the harms that targeted killings and signature strikes have on foreign populations (particularly civilians), they should also take up broader conceptual issues about the relationship between advanced military technologies and the legitimation of warfare. The Stockdale Center could also focus its energies on understanding decision-making in the use of unmanned weapon systems. There are many factors that lead to better decisions in the use of autonomous or semiautonomous systems. Time pressure, complexity, and responsibility are important variables in decision-making that need to be understood with reference to their moral and legal implications. This will involve an interdisciplinary approach that brings sociologists, ethicists, and applied psychologists to the drone debate.

The Stockdale Center could initiate another line of discourse about the potential moral and psychological harms that semiautonomous weapon systems have on the war fighters that operate them. Sparrow's analysis on the martial virtues might prove especially instructive in this case. He argues that these semiautonomous weapon systems undermine the cultivation of virtues such as courage due to the fact that they protect soldiers from enemy retaliation. Sparrow does not advocate placing soldiers in harm's way but does acknowledge that the age of drones is also an age in which the very character of being a soldier will undergo a massive transformation.[8] This transformation needs to be discussed in detail because it already seems to be having very real effects on the pilots who operate unmanned aerial systems. These individuals may be isolated in the civilian communities that often surround their bases, but also among their fellow soldiers, those who do not work with semi-autonomous aerial systems. Doing a better job of integrating drone pilots with more traditional military personnel may have the desired result of easing some of the stresses that drone operators experience and guarding against the adverse impacts of stress on decision-making. Additionally, more research needs to be conducted concerning the difference between the psychological strain experienced by these operators and the toll of traditional posttraumatic stress disorder (PTSD). This could be taken up more explicitly through the National Center for PTSD through the US Department of Veteran Affairs. Such research is not a reaction to a one-time or isolated turn in military affairs but should be understood as a first step in confronting the paradigm shift in war fighting that is currently occurring. In discussing the morality of drone warfare, it is necessary to remember the obligations that militaries have to protect soldiers and pilots, not only physically but also emotionally and morally.

The proliferation of drones

When it comes to the use of unmanned aerial systems, the United States is in an exceptional position, with relative hegemony over both the possession and use of the technology. As presented in chapter 2, the United States has been the predominant user of drones. Moreover, the number of drones used by the CIA and the US military has grown exponentially since 2001, with plans to double the number of medium- and high-altitude drones by 2021.[9] American preponderance will not always characterize the use of drones.

As we have suggested throughout the book, what makes drones attractive to the United States is already making them popular for export to and production in other countries. Seeing the political and economic – and indeed tactical – advantages that have driven the United States to expand their drone arsenal, the interest among other countries has intensified. All of the possible rivals to the United States are in the process of trying to acquire armed drones: China, Russia, and Iran. A world in which other countries possess drone technologies is quickly being created. Current defense journalist and former navy counter-electronic specialist Robert Densmore sums the situation up nicely: "We've always relied on [drones] as a force multiplier, a technological edge that we've had, [but] we've always known it wouldn't be a permanent advantage."[10]

Thus, perhaps the most important part of the drone story has to do with the proliferation of drones beyond the United States: what happens after other countries acquire drones?

What are the strategic or operational consequences? What can be done to stem the proliferation of drones? What types of institutional arrangements would be best suited to establishing norms for the appropriate uses of drones?

The first question deals with the security implications of other countries acquiring armed drones. According to the proliferation optimist camp, the consequences are few. Drones are just a different form of cruise missiles if it is the case that the technology will diffuse at all. Gilli and Gilli suggest that technological challenges will prevent drones from diffusing widely, particularly any drone that would qualify as anything other than a small UAV that would be used to swarm anti-aircraft systems, which requires a relatively rudimentary level of technology.[11] If the technology is not likely to diffuse widely, then the consequences of proliferation are not worth considering.

More persuasive is the proliferation pessimist perspective. To this point, the discussion of proliferation has been focused on the weapon systems that have dominated the US targeted killing program since 2001. This narrow focus has allowed us to describe the monopoly that the United States has over these military technologies. The United States is well ahead of the rest of the world when it comes to the infrastructure needed to employ advanced UAV systems. Recently, however, Brookings Institution expert Peter Singer observed that proliferation of drone technology in the coming decades will be defined by smaller and more versatile devices that do not require global satellite navigation. He states that it is necessary to remember that "We are no longer in a world where only the United States has the technology, and we are not moving toward a future in which the technology is used only in the same way we use it now."[12] The next century will witness the adoption of drone technologies in civilian airspace and this trend will allow state and non-state actors to acquire them with greater ease. Thus, one set of considerations deals with the smaller-scale drones that are inexpensive to produce and can proliferate easily, whether to individuals, non-state actors, or states. First, even these smaller-scale drones can have potentially serious consequences. One concern is that they can theoretically provide an inexpensive delivery system for weapons of mass destruction attacks by non-state groups. As the Government Accountability Office observed in 2004, drones "are ideally suited for the delivery of chemical and biological weapons given their ability to disseminate aerosols in appropriate locations at appropriate altitudes."[13] Navy Captain William Parker suggests that weaponizing anthrax might be difficult but aerosolizing VX or sarin is not.[14] Second, these small drones can also join forces into swarms, which can then overwhelm enemy air defenses; they could not do this individually but, collectively, with a hundred small drones, can swarm in a way that impedes another actor's ability to defend itself.[15] A third type of damage that small drones can inflict is as a kamikaze system which flies into its targets and does damage commensurate with its size.[16] The Israeli Harpy is this type of one-way system that essentially acts as a cruise missile flying into its target. Fourth, the deployment of even small drones can lead to miscalculation and unintended consequences. In September 2013, China flew a small, unarmed drone into the contested Senkaku Islands. As Brimley et al. observed after the incident, "the introduction of indigenous drones into Asia's strategic environment – now made official by China's maiden unmanned provocation – will bring with it additional sources of instability and escalation to the fiercely contested South and East China Seas."[17] Small unarmed aircraft deployed to another country's airspace can heighten tensions and increase the prospect of miscalculation with disproportionate consequences. As these examples – hypothetical and real-world – suggest, even small, inexpensive, and easily proliferated drones can produce important security consequences.

A further consideration deals with limited proliferation of more advanced drones. In this scenario, even the proliferation to a small set of countries could have large consequences. As mentioned before, all of the key international actors either have drones or are acquiring them. The numbers could be limited but the quantity is irrelevant if China, Russia, and Iran are the countries that possess them. Most fundamentally, if the risk-free nature of drones has lowered the threshold for conflict and expanded the battlefield in both space and time for the United States, the same will likely be true for other countries that acquire drones. The likelihood that these assets will come into contact and conflict with each other also increases as states expand their areas of operation. This would be especially problematic for sensitive regions such as East Asia, although it could also apply to Russia expanding its uses of armed assets in the Caucasus and Iran in the Middle East. Moreover, as these countries acquire drones, they will develop their own interpretations of appropriate targets for lethal drone strikes, with potentially destabilizing consequences that are very likely to contravene US interests.

Addressing this aspect of proliferation will require domestic drone manufactures to work closely with government officials to identify the security risks posed by the potential civilian–military crossover. In the next section on nonproliferation, we do not address this issue in great detail, instead focusing on the current international regimes that stand to limit the export of more advanced UAV systems. This focus is in line with limited objective of this volume, namely to think through the implications of the technologies currently used in combating asymmetric threats (primarily in the targeted-killing program).

Tools for nonproliferation and control of drones

As this analysis suggests, the United States currently has a monopoly in armed drones, but that window is closing quickly, and the consequences of proliferation are potentially serious, not just for American national security but for regional and international security. The question, then, is what to do about proliferation? We suggest a multipronged strategy. A first step would be to control and regulate the proliferation of drones through the judicious use of international law to establish arms control regulations on drones. According to Zenko's recent Council on Foreign Relations report, "[T]here is the reality that drones are proliferating but, as is often the case with new technologies, the international legal and regulatory framework is lagging behind."[18]

Currently, two primary international bodies govern the export of drones: the Missile Technology Control Regime (MTCR) and, to a lesser extent, the Wassenaar Arrangement. The MTCR is a voluntary association of thirty-four countries that controls the spread of ballistic and cruise missiles and armed drones. It divides drones into two categories: Category I drones exceed a range of 300 km and a payload of 500 kg and are strictly regulated in transfers; and Category II drones that are under these range and payload thresholds are subject to less stringent authorization for trade. Like the MTCR, the Wassenaar Arrangement is also a voluntary association. It includes forty-one countries that seek to limit the proliferation of munitions and sensitive dual-use items, items that have both military and civilian applications. The United States government has made three proposals to Wassenaar to reduce the proliferation of drones, which were all adopted. As a result, Wassenaar supplemented its control list with equipment that converts manned aircrafts to drones, drone guidance and control systems, and engines that power a drone above 50,000 feet. Wassenaar also updated and refined the control policy on various drones, such as navigation, altitude, and guidance and control systems. While the Wassenaar controls the export on many drones, it does not apply to all dual-use technologies that are critical to the development of drones. Due to the commercial applications of these technologies, however, they are difficult to add to the control list. From 2005 to 2011, MTCR members have adopted twenty-two drone-related technical controls, such as restrictions on turboprop systems used in Category I UAVs and inertial navigation in Category II UAVs. However, according to analysis by the US Government Accountability Office, "only 7 percent of UAV systems are subject to MTCR's strictest controls."[19] Unfortunately, by virtue of being geared toward technologies other than drones, the Wassenaar Arrangement and the MTCR leave gaps.

Those gaps also extend to the issue of participants themselves. Among states that are party to these organizations – including the United States – compliance with both agreements is strong; members have agreed to a strong "presumption of denial" of transfers and a "no undercut" policy in which they consult each other on exports prior to the transaction. In addition, large drone producers like the United States have been relatively attentive to the MTCR. Former Secretary of Defense Gates affirmed, "We are limited in what we can do by the MTCR,"[20] which means that exports of armed drones from the United States have been limited to just the United Kingdom.[21] According to State and Commerce Department officials, domestic controls on drones present in the Munitions and Commerce Control Lists are based on MTCR and Wassenaar controls. The United States also restricts the successive transfer of drones from countries it authorizes to export them (such as the United Kingdom) to other countries (for example, China) through end-user agreements.

Yet the result of these proliferation controls has been proliferation of nonmembers of the MTCR and Wassenaar controls. Israel has overtaken the United States as the largest exporter of drones, exporting US$4.6 billion between 2005 and 2012, mostly to Europe, Asia, or Latin America (and a large deal with India not included in these figures),[22] compared to US exports of US$2–3 billion. This difference exposes an important gap in the proliferation regime. Countries such as China, Russia, and Israel are not members of either association, which might reduce the ability for these international organizations to limit the spread of drones. Israel unilaterally adheres to the MTCR, but has nonetheless developed an enormous industry around exporting drones. As one individual involved in marketing at Israel Aerospace Industries observed, "we exist because of the international market. We're too big for Israel, to our delight," which is why 80 percent of its UAV production goes to consumers in the international market.[23] China's indigenous development of drone technology, combined with its history of arms exports and nonparticipation in international proliferation regimes, makes it a potential proliferation concern. As a Chinese aerospace spokesperson remarked, "The United States doesn't export many attack drones, so we're taking advantage of that hole in the market."[24]

One alternative to these existing regimes that are not drone-specific but rather have incorporated new drone technology is to create a drone-specific international institution such as the Nuclear Suppliers Group that would be organized to regulate drone manufacture and distribution. This international organization, made up of drone manufacturers around the world, would work closely with countries on the verge of acquiring drone technologies to ensure that they adopt certain best practices. Israel and the United States, being the principal producers of drones currently, would have to take the lead in this initiative. A less formal Proliferation Security

Initiative-like organization could also be a forum for regulating drone proliferation. By many accounts, the voluntary nature of the Proliferation Security Initiative has actually contributed to its success, drawing in countries that have mutual proliferation concerns but were averse to the constraints of a more formalized institution.[25] Additionally, we recognize that private–public partnerships, such as the Nuclear Threat Initiative (first developed by Sam Nunn and Ted Turner), could be an effective tool in bringing coordination among emerging drone powers.

A second strategy, which would not control drone exports but rather their use, is developing prudent precedent. As discussed in chapter 4, there are two main sources of international law: treaty law, which is positive law codified into formal, agreed-upon rules; and customary law, which is based upon state practice. The latter category is more difficult to assess since it requires considering the threshold at which practice becomes customary law, but the behavior of a powerful state is certainly a key influence on interpretations of customary law. Thus, how the United States uses drones today affects how others view the legitimate use of drones, potentially guiding future practices. With the long-term control of others' drone use in mind, the United States has strong incentives to limit the extent or circumstances of its own drone use. This move to self-regulate can have a positive impact on the ability to form coalitions in the international community. Gerald Dworkin wrote nearly thirty years ago that "An important consideration, to which little attention has been paid, is the role of restricting choices in symbolizing or expressing moral relationships,"[26] and indeed we might add instrumentally useful ones. A number of historical precedents point to the way that self-restraint in a period of hegemony can actually produce not just a moral precedent but one that serves the interests of that country over the longer term.

Immediately after World War II, the United States was in a position of hegemony compared to the rest of the world. Its economy was 50 percent of the world's gross domestic product and its military, particularly having demonstrated its monopoly over the development of the atom bomb, was similarly hegemonic. As Ikenberry notes, "at rare historical junctures, states grapple with the fundamental problem of international relations: how to create and maintain order in a world of sovereign states." In a world of power asymmetries, of strong and weak states, "hegemonic states face choices about how to use their newly acquired power."[27] In the post-World War II system, rather than exploiting its power advantages, the United States acted with "strategic restraint," establishing a liberal international order that in the short term limited its power and in the long term acted to "lock in" its leverage. The restraint came in part through limiting the extent to which it exercised power over other countries, giving others a vote in international institutions and being judicious in its use of force abroad.[28] In other words, the concentration of power is temporary and, by limiting the way in which it wields its power, a state can preserve it for the longer term, giving less powerful states institutional advantages that reassure them and give them incentives not to challenge the hegemon's power. In the case of drones, exercising restraint at this moment of techno-logical hegemony could pay dividends when drones become widespread. There are self-interested reasons why the United States should be concerned with establishing restraint and transparency about how it uses drones in combat. Another mechanism could be active norm development by the United States through semi-official channels. As Zenko notes, the United States could "promote Track 1.5 or Track 2 discussions on armed drones, similar to dialogues with other countries on the principles and limits of weapons systems such as nuclear weapons or cyberwarfare." The approaches are both unilaterial – modifying its own drone policy – and multilateral through international cooperation but could help stem, or at least regulate, the distribution of drones and how that technology is used in the future.

Concluding remarks

The authors of this book are neither Luddites nor peaceniks. We understand and take seriously the realist concerns about the dangers of twenty-first century international relations, specifically transnational terrorism. At the same time, however, we strongly believe that these dangers can be addressed without jettisoning enduring legal or moral principles. In this regard, we end up somewhere between realism and pacifism on the ideological spectrum, in the middle ground where just war theory and international humanitarian law holds sway.

Methodologically, we are generally pragmatists. Pragmatists hold that situations (political, legal, and moral) should be judged carefully on a case-by-case basis. They are loath to adopt a one-solution-fits-all approach to international affairs and deeply suspicious of policies that seem to do so. Nonetheless, pragmatism is not the same as adopting an anything-goes mentality that applies haphazardly to a wide array of principles in situations as they arise. Toward this end, we acknowledge that counterterrorism strategies need to remain flexible and that drones will facilitate this flexibility in coming years.

The drone age is upon us and we welcome the obvious advantages that modern military technology such as drones provide in fighting just wars. In particular, we welcome drones' ability to minimize bloodshed – and especially civilian casualties – as compared with previous military technologies such as strategic bombing. But while acknowledging the benefits of drones, the mission of this book was to highlight the subtle dangers that coexist, and in some cases stem from, drones' advantages. In particular: The rhetoric and moral thinking about war has become sloppier as our weaponry has become more precise. Our reliance on precision weaponry risks becoming a stand-in for hard moral or legal decisions. Combatant status cannot be determined by an algorithm, and we should not be lulled into believing that technical precision can extricate us from complicated questions. Instead, we should recognize the unshakably human character of war and identify new ethical and legal resources to regulate armed conflict.

Restating and maintaining the human character of war will not be easy in an age of advanced military devices. Indeed, some scholars have argued that it is not even preferable. We should let the robots do our fighting, they argue, because, after all, they have nothing to lose. But we do. When robots become our mercenaries, we stand to lose the sense that war has costs, even if indirect ones. These costs – and especially the moral costs – are often slow in showing themselves, so slow that it is often too late to mitigate them when they finally appear. These costs are not indirect, abstract, or irrelevant if they affect people half a world away. This book's primary aim is to make these costs known to the citizens whose governments employ modern military technologies abroad in their name.

Notes

CHAPTER I   INTRODUCTION: THE RISE OF DRONES

1 Alex Rodriguez, "Clinton's Pakistan Visit Reveals Widespread Distrust of US," *LA Times*, November 1, 2009.

2 "Clinton faces Pakistani Anger at Drone Attacks." Quoted by Fox News, October 30, 2009.

3 Mary Bruce, "Drone Strikes on US Terror Suspects 'Legal,' 'Ethical,' 'Wise,' White House Says," *ABC News*, February 5, 2013.

4 Colin Kahl, "In the Crossfire or in the Crosshairs? Norms, Civilians, and US Conduct in Iraq," *International Security* 32(1) (2007): 7–46.

5 New America Foundation. Available at natsec.newamerica.net/, last accessed January 9, 2014.

6 "US Drone Strikes Listed and Detailed in Pakistan, Somalia and Yemen," *The Guardian*, August 2, 2012.

7 Richard Van Atta et al., 2003, *Transformation and Transition: DARPA's Role in Fostering an Emerging Revolution in Military Affairs*, Arlington, VA: Institute for Defense Analysis, S-8, S-9.

8 Jeremy Scahill, 2013, *Dirty Wars: The World is a Battlefield*, New York: Perseus Books.

9 Quoted in Jane Mayer, "The Predator War," *New Yorker*, October 26, 2009.

10 Cofer Black, "Joint Investigation into September 11 Attacks," quoted in *Top Secret America*, PBS. Frontline TV production published Sept. 11, 2011.

11 Micah Zenko, "10 Things You Didn't Know about Drones," *Foreign Policy*, February 12, 2012.

12 Mark Mazzetti, 2013, *The Way of the Knife: The CIA, a Secret Army, and a War at the Ends of the Earth*, Penguin Press.

13 John Sifton, "A Brief History of Drones," *The Nation*, February 7, 2012.

14 This number does not include small UAVs, micro UAVs, or lighter-than-air platforms, nor does it include CIA platforms. See Jeremiah Gertler, "US Unmanned Aerial Systems," report, Washington DC: Congressional Research Service, pp. 7–8.

15 Audrey Kurth Cronin, "Why Drones Fail," *Foreign Affairs*, July/August 2013.

16 See, for example, John Mueller, 1985, *War, Presidents, and Public Opinion*, University Press of America; though Peter Feaver, Christopher Gelpi, and Jason Reifler challenge the notion that casualties reduce the popularity of conflict. See *Paying the Human Costs of War*, 2009, Princeton University Press.

17 Fairleigh Dickinson University poll fielded December 10–16, 2012, asking "in what country are those attacks most concentrated?"

18 To the best of your knowledge, can the US target US citizens living in other countries with drones, or is that illegal? Fairleigh Dickinson University, February 7, 2013; in general, do you approve or disapprove of the US military using drones to carry out attacks abroad on people and other targets deemed a threat to the United States?

19 Carol Cratty and Joe Johns, "Holder: Drone Strikes Have Killed Four Americans since 2009," CNN, May 23, 2013.

20 *Nonproliferation: Agencies Could Improve Information Sharing and End-Use Monitoring on Unmanned Aerial Vehicle Exports*, 2012. Washington, DC: General Accounting Office.

21 Frank Herbert, 1965, *Dune*, NY: Chilton Books; Isaac Asimov, 1982, *The Complete Robot*, NY: Doubleday.

22 Micah Zenko, "Reforming US Drone Strike Policies," *Council on Foreign Relations*, Special Report 65 (2013) [14].

23 "Remarks at a Meeting with the American Society of Newspaper Editors," April 17, 1947. Available at www.trumanlibrary.org.

24 Jens David Ohlin, 2012, "Targeting Co-Belligerents," in *Targeted Killings: Law and Morality in an Asymmetrical World*, New York: Oxford University Press, p. 68; Robert Sparrow, "Building a Better WarBot: Ethical Issues in the Design of Unmanned Systems for Military Applications," *Science and Engineering Ethics* 15(2) (2009): 169–87; Ronald Arkin, 2011, "Governing Legal Behavior: Embedding Ethics in a Hybrid Deliberative/Reactive Robot Architecture," GVU Technical Report GIT-GVU-07–11;

Bradley Strawser, "Moral Predators: The Duty to Employ Uninhabited Aerial Vehicles," *Journal of Military Ethics* 9(4) (2010): 342–68. For a detailed analysis of the relationship between ethics and technology, please see John Kaag and Whitley Kaufman, "Military Frameworks: Technological Know-how and the Legitimation of Modern Warfare," *Cambridge Review of International Affairs* 22(4) (2009): 585–606.

25 Michael Walzer, "Political Action: The Problem of Dirty Hands," *Philosophy and Public Affairs* 2(2) (Winter 1973): 160–80.

26 "The United States in the World – Just Wars and Just Societies: An Interview with Michael Walzer," *Imprints: A Journal of Analytical Socialism* 7(1) (2003).

27 We differentiate between the use of drones in the context of active combat, such as Afghanistan, and for counterterrorism in Yemen, Pakistan, and Somalia, which we argue in chapter 4 are more problematic than in the context of active conflict.

28 Leon Panetta, 2009, Speech at the Pacific Council on International Security. Retrieved from "US airstrikes in Pakistan called 'very effective,'" CNN.

CHAPTER 2   THE NUTS AND BOLTS OF DRONES

1 "CIA 'Killed Al-Qaeda Suspects' in Yemen," BBC, November 5, 2002.

2 "US Predator Kills 6 Al Qaeda Suspects," ABC News, November 5, 2002.

3 President Barack Obama, "Remarks by the President at the National Defense University," May 23, 2013. Available at www.whitehouse.gov/the-press-office/2013/05/23/remarks-president-national-defense-university, last accessed January 9, 2014.

4 "The US and Unmanned Flight – Part I." *Airforce-Technology.com*, January 25, 2008.

5 We thank an anonymous reviewer and Colonel Rob Spalding, Council on Foreign Relations military fellow, for making this point. See also John Villasenor, "What is a Drone, Anyway?" *Scientific American*, April 12, 2012.

6 "DIY Drones: Don't Confuse Homemade UAVs with Military Killing Machines," *The Guardian*, May 24, 2013.

7 General Accounting Office, *Nonproliferation*, 13, July 30, 2013.

Available at www.gao.gov/products/GAO-12–536, last accessed January 13, 2014.

8 "The US and Unmanned Flight – Part I." *Airforce-Technology. com*, January 25, 2008.

9 John Villasenor, "High-Altitude Surveillance Drones: Coming to a Sky Near You," *Scientific American*, February 24, 2012.

10 For example, low-caliber surface-to-air artillery and Man Portable Air Defense Systems (Manpads).

11 Graham Warwick, "Aurora's Orion MALE UAV Aims for 120-Hr. Flight," *Defense Week*, September 17, 2013.

12 Derek Gregory, "From a View to a Kill: Drones and Late Modern War," *Theory, Culture & Society* 28(7–8) (2011): 188–215.

13 Available at http://news.cnet.com/8301–13578_3–57572207–38/ dhs-built-domestic-surveillance-tech-into-predator-drones/, last accessed January 9, 2014.

14 Thomas McDonnell, "Sow What You Reap? Using Predator and Reaper Drones to Carry out Assassinations or Targeted Killings of Suspected Islamic Terrorists," *George Washington International Law Review* 44 (2012).

15 Available at www.af.mil/information/factsheets/index.asp, last accessed January 9, 2014.

16 See MQ-9 Reaper, 111th Fighter Wing. Available at www.111fw. ang.af.mil/resources/, last accessed January 9, 2014.

17 Joshua Foust and Ashley Boyle, *The Strategic Context of Lethal Drones: A Framework for Discussion*, Washington, DC: American Security Project; see table 1, p. 4.

18 Air Force F-22 Fighter Program, Congressional Research Service, 2013, 9; Defense Acquisitions: Assessments of Selected Weapon Programs, March 2013, Washington, DC: Government Accountability Office.

19 Armin Krishnan, 2009, *Killer Robots: Legality and Ethicality of Autonomous Weapons*, Burlington, VT: Ashgate, p. 64.

20 Aram Roston, "Will Congress Let the Air Force Abandon the Global Hawk?" *Defense News*, June 24, 2013.

21 John Reed, "Predator Drones 'Useless' in Most Wars, Top Air Force General Says," *Foreign Policy*, September 29, 2013.

22 Sydney Freedberg Jr, "Drones Need Secure Datalinks to Survive vs Iran, China," *Breaking Defense*, August 10, 2012.

23 Michael Lewis, "Drones and the Boundaries of the Battlefield." *Texas International Law Journal* 47(2) (2011): 293–314.

24 For a discussion of differences between Title 10 and Title 50, see Andru Wall, "Demystifying the Title 10-Title 50 Debate: Distinguishing Military Operations, Intelligence Activities & Covert Action," *Harvard National Security Journal* 3 (2011). See also Robert Chesney, "Military-Intelligence Convergence and the Law of the Title 10/Title 50 Debate," *Journal of National Security Law and Policy* 5 (2012): 539–629.

25 Chris Woods and Alice Ross, "Revealed: US and Britain Launched 1,200 Drone Strikes in Recent Wars," December 4, 2012. Available at www.thebureauinvestigates.com/2012/12/04/revealed-us-and-britain-launched-1200-drone-strikes-in-recent-wars/, last accessed January 15, 2014.

26 Alice Ross, "UK Drones Three Times More Likely than US to Fire in Afghanistan," Bureau of Investigative Journalism, September 6, 2013.

27 Chris Woods and Alice Ross, "Revealed: US and Britain Launched 1,200 Drone Strikes in Recent Wars."

28 Mark Mazzetti and Eric Schmitt, "US Expands its Drone War into Somalia," *New York Times*, July 1, 2011.

29 Philip Victor, "Pakistan PM Uses UN Address to Press US Over Drone Strikes," Al Jazeera, September 27, 2013.

30 Greg Miller and Bob Woodward, "Secret Memos Reveal Explicit Nature of US, Pakistan Agreement on Drones," *Washington Post*, October 24, 2013.

31 Michael Gordon, "Kerry, in Pakistan, Expresses Optimism on Ending Drone Strikes Soon," *New York Times*, August 1, 2013.

32 Jonathan Masters and Zachary Laub, "Al-Qaeda in the Arabian Peninsula," Council on Foreign Relations, August 22, 2013.

33 Mohammed Hatem and Caroline Alexander, "Al-Qaeda Suspects Die in Stepped-Up Yemen Drone Strikes," *Bloomberg*, August 9, 2013.

34 Tracy McVeigh, "Investigation to Record Victims of US Drone Attacks in Pakistan," *The Guardian*, September 21, 2013.

35 See Jack Goldsmith and Eric Posner, "A Theory of Customary International Law," *The University of Chicago Law Review* 66(4) (Autumn 1999): 1113–77; 1113.

36 Micah Zenko, "Reforming US Drone Strike Policies," *Council on Foreign Relations*, Special Report 65 (2013) [14].

37 Greg Miller, "White House Approves Broader Yemen Drone Campaign." *Washington Post*, April 25, 2012; Kevin Jon Heller,

"'One Hell of a Killing Machine.' Signature Strikes and International Law," *Journal of International Criminal Justice* 11(1) (2013): 89–119.

38 RT.com., "Classified documents reveal CIA drone strikes often killed unknown people," June 7, 2013.

39 Julian Barnes, "US Relaxes Drone Rules," *The Wall Street Journal*, April 26, 2012.

40 "Fact Sheet: US Policy Standards and Procedures for the Use of Force in Counterterrorism Operations Outside the United States and Areas of Active Hostilities," May 23, 2013. Available at www.whitehouse.gov/the-press-office/2013/05/23/fact-sheet-us-policy-standards-and-procedures-use-force-counterterrorism, last accessed January 9, 2014.

41 Micah Zenko, "Reforming US Drone Strike Policies."

42 Department of Justice White Paper, 2011, "Lawfulness of a Lethal Operation Directed Against a US Citizen Who is a Senior Operational Leader of Al-Qa'ida or An Associated Force." NBC News, 2013.

43 Department of Justice White Paper, 2011, "Lawfulness of a Lethal Operation Directed Against a US Citizen Who is a Senior Operational Leader of Al-Qa'ida or An Associated Force." NBC News, 2013; Trevor McCrisken, "Obama's Drone War," *Survival: Global Politics and Strategy* 55(2) (2013): 97–122.

44 See, for example, "Al Libi Taken to New York Week after Capture in Libya," CNN, October 15, 2013.

45 "Plan for Hunting Terrorists Signals US Intends to Keep Adding Names to Kill Lists," *Washington Post*, October 23, 2012.

46 Mark Mazzetti, "Origins of CIA's Not-So-Secret Drone War in Pakistan," *New York Times*, April 6, 2013.

47 Mark Mazzetti, 2013, *The Way of the Knife: The CIA, A Secret Army, and a War at the Ends of the Earth*, Penguin Press.

48 John T. Bennett, "McCain, Feinstein Split over Shifting Strike UAV Program to Military," *Defense News*, March 21, 2013.

49 Jack Goldsmith, "The Way of the Knife Review," *LAWFARE*, May 1, 2013.

50 Trevor McCrisken, "Obama's Drone War," *Survival: Global Politics and Strategy* 55(2) (2013): 97–122.

51 Scott Shane, "Election Spurred a Move to Codify US Drone Policy," *The New York Times*, November 24, 2012.

52 Tara McKelvey, "Media Coverage of the Drone Program," Joan
    Shorenstein Center on the Press, Politics, and Public Policy
    Cambridge, MA: 2013, p. 1. Available at http://shorensteincenter.
    org/2013/02/media-coverage-of-the-drone-program/, last
    accessed January 9, 2014.

53 It is worth mentioning that, as Mazzetti describes, a private
    and informal *quid pro quo* may have developed between the
    Obama Administration and Pakistani officials whereby the
    Obama Administration received tacit or implicit permission to
    conduct certain drone operations that targeted high-value US
    targets if drone strikes were also conducted to target militants
    who threatened Pakistani security. UN Special Rapporteur on
    Counter-Terrorism and Human Rights, 2013, "Statement of
    the Special Rapporteur Following Meetings in Pakistan," United
    Nations Office of the High Commissioner for Human Rights.

54 Owen Bowcott, "UN to Investigate Civilian Deaths from US
    Drone Strikes," *The Guardian*, October 25, 2012.

55 ACLU, Amnesty International, Center for Human Rights &
    Global Justice, NYU School of Law, Center for Civilians in
    Conflict, Center for Constitutional Rights, Global Justice Clinic,
    NYU School of Law, Human Rights First, Human Rights
    Institute, Columbia Law School, Human Rights Watch, Open
    Society Foundations, 2013, "Joint Letter to President Obama on
    US Drone Strikes and Targeted Killings."

56 Caroline Kennedy and Nicholas Rengger, "The New
    Assassination Bureau: On the 'Robotic Turn' in Contemporary
    War," *Carnegie Ethics*, November 6, 2012.

57 "White House Responds to Drone Pressure: 'We Will Continue
    to Disclose as Much as We Can,'" *McClatchy*, April 12, 2013.

58 Greg Miller, "Brennan Speech is First Obama Acknowledgement
    of Use of Armed Drones." *The Washington Post*, April 30,
    2012.

59 David Jackson, "Obama Outlines Counterterrorism Policy," *USA
    Today*, May 23, 2013.

60 Tom Cohen and Tom Watkins, "Another US Citizen a Potential
    Drone Target", CNN, February 11, 2014.

61 Office of the Press Secretary, 2013, "Fact Sheet: US
    Policy Standards and Procedures for the Use of Force in
    Counterterrorism Operations outside the United States and
    Areas of Active Hostilities." Available at *WhiteHouse.gov*.

62 Kenneth Anderson, "You are an Operational Commander of AQAP Reading the White House Fact Sheet," *Lawfare*, May 24, 2013.

63 Jack Goldsmith, "How Obama Undermined the War on Terror: The President Promised Not to Undercut the Rule of Law for Expedience's Sake. He Did. Now We Face the Consequences," *New Republic*, May 1, 2013.

64 As we discuss in chapter 3, the strikes ostensibly draw their domestic legal authorization from the Authorization for the Use of Military Force (AUMF), which allows the president "to use all necessary and appropriate force against those nations, organizations, or persons he determines planned, authorized, committed, or aided the terrorist attacks that occurred on September 11, 2011, or harbored such organizations or persons, in order to prevent any future acts of international terrorism against the United States by such nations, organizations, or persons." This includes members of al-Qaeda, the Taliban, or associated forces, regardless of their presence in official battlefields like Afghanistan or nonmilitarized zones like Pakistan. However, it does not speak to the targeting criteria, which we suggest in chapter 4 is based on debatable claims.

65 Greg Miller, "Brennan Speech is First Obama Acknowledgement of Use of Armed Drones," *The Washington Post*, April 30, 2012.

66 Cora Currier and Justin Elliott, "The Drone War Doctrine We Still Know Nothing About," *ProPublica*, February 26, 2013.

67 Ibid.

68 Dennis Gormley, "Limiting the Unintended Consequences of Unmanned Air System Proliferation," *The Whitehead Journal of Diplomacy and International Relations* 14(1) (2013): 67–79.

69 Government Accountability Office, 2012, *NonProliferation: Agencies Could Improve Information Sharing and End-Use Monitoring on Unmanned Aerial Vehicle Exports*, Washington, DC.

70 David Schenker, "How the Israeli Drone Strike in the Sinai Might Backfire," *The Atlantic*, August 13, 2013; Fares Akram and Isabel Kershner, "Israeli Drone Strike Kills Militants in Southern Gaza," *New York Times*, October 29, 2011.

71 Alice Ross, "UK Drones Three Times More Likely than US to Fire in Afghanistan," The Bureau of Investigative Journalism, September 6, 2013.

72 See *Jane's UAV Technology Review*, 2011.

73 Brad Knickerbocker, "US considered missions to destroy RQ-170 Sentinel drone lost in Iran," *Christian Science Monitor*, December 7, 2011.

74 Kristina Wong, "US Drone a Tech Challenge for Iran," *Washington Times*, January 12, 2012.

75 "China Urged to Stop Drone Flights Near Senkaku Islands," *Japan Times*, September 10, 2013.

76 Barack Obama, 2013, "President Obama's Speech at National Defense University: The Future of our Fight against Terrorism," Council on Foreign Relations. Dan Byman, "Why Drones Work," *Foreign Affairs* (July/August 2013): 32–43.

77 "Living Under Drones. Strategic Considerations," Stanford Law School. Available at www.livingunderdrones.org/report-strategy/#_ftn6, last accessed January 9, 2014.

78 Joshua Foust, 2013, "Understanding the Strategic and Tactical Considerations of Drone Strikes," *American Security Project* 2. Available at http://americansecurityproject.org/ASP%20Reports/Ref%200110%20-%20Understanding%20the%20Strategic%20and%20Tactical%20Considerations%20of%20Drone%20Strikes.pdf, last accessed January 9, 2014.

79 For a discussion of selection bias in the context of decapitation, see Patrick Johnston, "Does Decapitation Work? Assessing the Effectiveness of Leadership Targeting in Counterinsurgency Campaigns," *International Security* 36(4) (Spring 2012): 47–79.

80 Patrick Johnston, "Does Decapitation Work?"

81 Bryan Price, "Targeting Top Terrorists: How Leadership Decapitation Contributes to Counterterrorism," *International Security* 36(4) (Spring 2012): 9–46.

82 Kent Layne Oots, "Bargaining with Terrorists: Organizational Considerations," *Terrorism* 13(2) (March/April 1990): 145–58.

83 Joshua Foust, "Understanding the Strategic and Tactical Considerations of Drone Strikes," *American Security Project* 13 (2013). Available at http://americansecurityproject.org/featured-items/2013/understanding-the-strategic-and-tactical-considerations-of-drone-strikes/, last accessed January 9, 2014.

84 Pir Zubair Shah, 2012, "My Drone War," *Foreign Policy* (March/April).

85 Peter Baker, "In Terror Shift, Obama Took a Long Path," *New York Times*, May 27, 2013.

86 Anonymous interview with the author, July 16, 2013.

87 Audrey Kurth Cronin, "Why Drones Fail," *Foreign Affairs*, July/August 2013.

88 David Kilcullen and Andrew Exum, "Death from Above, Outrage Down Below," *New York Times*, May 16, 2009.

89 Audrey Kurth Cronin, "How al-Qaida Ends: The Decline and Demise of Terrorist Groups," *International Security* 31(1) (Summer 2006): 7–48; 22.

90 Pew Research, 2013, "Global Opinion of Obama Slips, International Policies Faulted," Pew Research Global Attitudes Project.

91 Letta Tayler, 2012, "Losing Yemeni Hearts and Minds," *Human Rights Watch*. Salon.

92 Tom Hussain, "Pakistan's Nawaz Sharif Declares End to Secret Approval of US Drone Strikes," *Miami Herald*, June 10, 2013.

93 Pew Research Global Attitudes Project, ch. 1: "Attitudes Toward the United States," July 18, 2013.

94 "Drop the Pilot," *Economist*, October 19, 2013.

95 Micah Zenko, "Reforming US Drone Strike Policies," 10; Craig Whitlock, "Flow of Terrorist Recruits Increasing," *The Washington Post*, October 19, 2009.

96 Jenna Jordan, "When Heads Roll: Assessing the Effectiveness of Leadership Decapitation," *Security Studies* 18 (2009): 719–55; 748.

97 UN Special Rapporteur on Counter-Terrorism and Human Rights, 2013, "Statement of the Special Rapporteur Following Meetings in Pakistan," United Nations Office of the High Commissioner for Human Rights.

98 UN Special Rapporteur on Counter-Terrorism and Human Rights, 2013, "Statement of the Special Rapporteur Following Meetings in Pakistan," United Nations Office of the High Commissioner for Human Rights.

99 "Generation Kill: A Conversation with Stanley McChrystal," *Foreign Affairs*, March/April 2013.

100 Jason Koebler, "Administration Saw Drone Strikes as 'Cure-All' for Terrorism," *US News*, May 23, 2013.

CHAPTER 3   DRONES AND DEMOCRACY

1 Many of the ideas from this section first appeared in John Kaag
   and Sarah Kreps, "Drones and Democratic Peace," *Brown Journal
   of World Affairs* 19(2) (Spring/Summer 2013).
2 Immanuel Kant, 2001, "Towards Perpetual Peace," *The Basic
   Writings of Kant*, ed. Allen Wood, New York: Random House,
   p. 422.
3 Ibid.
4 Benjamin Valentino, Paul Huth, and Sarah Croco, "Bear Any
   Burden? How Democracies Minimize the Costs of War," *Journal
   of Politics* 72(2) (Apr. 2010): 528–44, 528.
5 Dan Reiter and Allan Stam, 2002, *Democracies at War*, Princeton
   University Press.
6 Matthew Evangelista, *Unarmed Forces*, Ithaca, NY: Cornell
   University Press.
7 BBC, "On this Day: 18 April, 1960."
8 Henry David Thoreau, 1937, *Works of Thoreau*, ed. Henry S.
   Canby, Boston: Houghton Mifflin.
9 John Kaag and Sarah Kreps, "Drones and Democratic Peace,"
   Brown Journal of World Affairs 19(11) (Spring/Summer).
10 Paul Kahn, "The Paradox of Riskless War," *Philosophy and Public
   Policy Quarterly* 22(3) (2002): 2–8.
11 Immanuel Kant, 2001, "Towards Perpetual Peace," in the *Basic
   Writings of Kant*, ed. Allen Wood, New York: Random House.
12 Gustavo Flores-Macias and Sarah Kreps, "Political Parties at
   War: A Study of American War Finance 1789–2010," *American
   Political Science Review* 11(4) (2013): 833–48.
13 "Big Tax Bill Passed," *Washington Post*, February 14, 1919, p. 1.
14 John Kaag and Sarah Kreps, "Drones and Democratic Peace,"
   Brown Journal of World Affairs 19(2) (Spring/Summer 2013).
15 Harlan Geer, 2005, *Unmanned Aerial Vehicles: Background and
   Issues for Congress*, Washington, DC: Congressional Research
   Service, p. 9.
16 Jeremiah Gertler, "US Unmanned Aerial Systems," Washington,
   DC: Congressional Research Service, p. 10.
17 W. J. Hennigan, "US May Rely on Aging U-2 Spy Planes Longer
   than Expected," *LA Times*, January 28, 2012.
18 A Tucano is a Brazilian-made aircraft used for counterinsurgency

or close air support. "UAVs Cost-Effectiveness is Compelling Argument," *Defence IQ Press*, January 28, 2010.

19 Peter Singer, "Do Drones Undermine Democracy?" *New York Times*, January 21, 2012.

20 Elizabeth Bone and Christopher Bolkcom, 2003, *Unmanned Aerial Vehicles: Background and Issues for Congress*, Washington, DC: Congressional Research Service.

21 Phillip Everts, 2001, *Public Opinion and the International Use of Force*, London: Routledge, p. 18.

22 "Unmanned Aerial Vehicles (Drones): An Introduction," UK Parliament briefing. Available at www.parliament.uk/briefing-papers/SN06493.pdf, last accessed January 9, 2014.

23 New America Foundation, The Year of the Drone. Available at http://counterterrorism.newamerica.net/drones, last accessed January 9, 2014.

24 Fairleigh Dickinson University poll fielded December 10–16, 2012, asking "how much have you heard or read about these drones?"

25 Fairleigh Dickinson University poll fielded December 10–16, 2012, asking "in what country are those attacks most concentrated?"

26 Chris Cillizza, "The American Public Loves Drones," *The Washington Post*, February 6, 2013.

27 One minor exception is the June 2013 question about whether individuals are concerned with oversight of the drone program, with 66 percent of Americans suggesting that they are somewhat or very concerned. (CBS/NYT 6/6/2013).

28 "Voters are Gung-Ho for Use of Drones but Not over the United States," Rasmussen, February 13, 2012.

29 Kenneth Anderson, *Targeted Killing in US Counterterrorism Strategy and Law* 7 (Series on Counterterrorism and American Statutory Law, Working Paper, May 11, 2009).

30 Mazzetti, quoted in Stephen Holmes, "What's in It for Obama?" *London Review of Books*, July 18, 2013.

31 Holmes, ibid.

32 Mazzetti, quoted in Jack Goldsmith, "How Obama Undermined the War on Terror," *New Republic*, May 1, 2013.

33 Jo Becker and Scott Shane, "Secret 'Kill List' Tests Obama's Principles," *New York Times*, May 29, 2012.

34 Charlie Savage and Mark Landler, "War Powers Act Doesn't Apply for Libya, Obama Says," *New York Times*, June 15, 2011.

35 Michael Crowley, "Revisiting a Key Legal Basis for Obama's Drone Strikes," *Time*, June 12, 2012.

36 50 USC (US Code), ch.33, War Powers Resolution. Available at www.law.cornell.edu/uscode/text/50/chapter-33, last accessed January 12, 2014.

37 Bruce Ackerman, "President Obama: Don't Go There," *Washington Post*, April 20, 2012.

38 "Obama Wants to End 'War on Terror' but Congress Balks," *Reuters*, 24 May, 2013.

39 Council on Foreign Relations, Council Special Report 65.

40 James Q. Wilson, 1989, *Bureaucracy: What Government Agencies Do and Why They Do It*, New York, NY: Basic Books.

41 Kenneth Schultz, 2003, "Tying Hands and Washing Hands: The US Congress and Multilateral Humanitarian Intervention," in Daniel Drezner (ed.), *Locating the Proper Authorities: The Interaction of International and Domestic Institutions*, Ann Arbor, MI: University of Michigan Press, pp. 105–42.

42 Amy Zegart, 1999, *Flawed by Design: The Evolution of the CIA, JCS, and NSC*, Stanford, CA: Stanford University Press, p. 10.

43 Scott Shane and Michael Shear, "Visions of Drones Swarming US Skies Hit Bipartisan Nerve," *New York Times*, March 8, 2013.

44 Jane Mayer, "Torture and Obama's Drone Program," *New Yorker*, February 15, 2013.

45 Pierre Thomas and Chris Good, "US Says 4 Americans Killed by Drones in Counterterror Strikes," *ABC News*, May 22, 2013.

46 Scott Shane, "Debating a Court to Vet Drone Strikes," *New York Times*, February 8, 2013.

47 Scott Shane, "Judge Challenges White House Claims on Authority in Drone Killings," *New York Times*, July 19, 2013.

48 Rachel Martin, "How a 'Drone Court' Might Work," *NPR*, March 31, 2013.

49 Quoted in Stephen Vladeck, "Al-Awlaqi and the Futility (and Utility) of Bivens Suits in National Security Cases," *American Constitution Society* blog, July 23, 2013.

50 Judge from the US District Court for the Southern District of New York, quoted in Daphne Eviatar, "The Secrecy Veiling Obama's Drone War," *Reuters*, January 4, 2013.

51 Jane Harman, "Drone Courts Can Work," Wilson Center, CNN, February 19, 2013.

52 Gabor Rona, "The Pro-rule of Law Argument against a 'Drone Court,'" *The Hill*, May 27, 2013.

53 Joe Wolverton, "Congress Considers Special Drone Court; UN Investigates Deadly Drone Strikes," *The New American*, February 14, 2013.

54 Neal Katyal, "An Executive Branch 'Drone Court,'" *New York Times*, February 20, 2013.

55 Katyal, "An Executive Branch 'Drone Court.'"

56 Deborah Pearlstein, "These Aren't the Courts We're Looking For," *Opinio Juris*, February 15, 2013.

57 *Al-Aulaqi v. Obama*, 727 F. Supp.2d 1, 45 (D. D.C. 2010) (quoting *DaCosta v. Laird*, 471 F.2d 1146, 1155 (2d Cir. 1973)).

58 Joe Wolverton, "Congress Considers Special Drone Court; UN Investigates Deadly Drone Strikes," *The New American*, February 14, 2013.

59 Jeh Johnson, "Keynote address at the Center on National Security at Fordham Law School," *Lawfare Blog*, March 18, 2013. Available at www.lawfareblog.com/2013/03/jeh-johnson-speech-on-a-drone-court-some-pros-and-cons/, last accessed January 9, 2014.

60 Barack Obama, "President Obama Gives a Speech on National Security at the National Defense University," *CNN*, May 23, 2013.

61 Eric Lichtblau, "In Secret, Court Vastly Broadens Powers of NSA," *New York Times*, July 6, 2013.

62 Ibid.

63 Ibid.

64 Mark Hosenball, "Support Grows for US 'Drone Court' to Review Lethal Strikes," *Reuters*, February 8, 2013.

65 "A Second Opinion on Drone Strikes," *LA Times*, February 18, 2013.

66 See Neal Katyal, "An Executive Branch 'Drone Court,'" *New York Times*, 20 February 2013, among others.

67 Steve Coll, "Kill or Capture: Obama's Troubling Targeted-Killing Policy," *New Yorker*, August 2, 2012.

68 Michael Walzer, interview, "Michael Walzer on Just War Theory," Big Think, http://bigthink.com/ideas/1526, last accessed January 9, 2014.

CHAPTER 4   DRONES AND INTERNATIONAL LAW

1 Michael Isikoff, "Justice Department memo Reveals Case for Drone Strikes on Americans," *NBC News*, February 4, 2013.

2 Attorney General Eric Holder Speaks at Northwestern University School of Law, March 5, 2012; for a representative view of the critics, see Eric Posner, "President Obama Can Do Anything He Wants on Terrorism," *Slate*, February 5, 2013.

3 Martha Finnemore and Kathryn Sikkink, "International Norm Dynamics and Political Change," *International Organization* 52(4) (1998): 887–917: Emilie Hafner-Burton, "Sticks and Stones: Naming and Shaming the Human Rights Enforcement Problem," *International Organization* 62(4) (2008): 689–716.

4 Nicholas Wheeler, "Dying for 'Enduring Freedom': Accepting Responsibility for Civilian Casualties in the War on Terrorism," *International Relations* 16 (2002): 205–25, 210.

5 Michael W. Lewis, "The Law of Aerial Bombardment in the 1991 Gulf War," *American Journal of International Law* 97(3) (July 2003): 481–509.

6 David Mets, 2001, *The Long Search for a Surgical Strike: Precision Munitions and the Revolution in Military Affairs*, Montgomery, AL: Air University Press, p. 39.

7 Lt. Gen. Buster Glosson, "Impact of Precision Weapons on Air Combat Operations," *Airpower Journal* (Summer 1993): 4–10.

8 Harold Koh, "The Obama Administration and International Law," *Annual Meeting of the American Society of International Law*, Washington, DC: United States Department of State, 2010.

9 Report of the Special Rapporteur on Extrajudicial, Summary or Arbitrary Executions, Human Rights Council, May 28, 2010.

10 O'Connell notes that states can also use force to suppress rebel uprisings or if a state has been invited to suppress an uprising. These latter two circumstances do not seem germane in terms of the use of drones. See Mary Ellen O'Connell, "Remarks: The Resort to Drones under International Law," *Denver Journal of International Law* 585(39) (2010–11): 585–600.

11 Anthony Arend, "International Law and the Preemptive Use of Military Force," *The Washington Quarterly* 26(2) (Spring 2003): 89–103.

12 Nicholas Wheeler and Alex Bellamy, 2008, "Humanitarian

Intervention in World Politics," in John Baylis and Steve Smith (eds), *The Globalization of World Politics: An Introduction to International Relations*, Oxford: Oxford University Press, pp. 522–39.

13 Michael Glennon, *Limits of Law, Prerogatives of Power: Interventionism after Kosovo* (Palgrave: 2001); Alex Bellamy, 2008, "Pre-Empting Terror," in *Security and the War on Terror*, New York: Routledge.

14 Harold Koh, "The Obama Administration and International Law."

15 Robert Chesney, "Postwar," *Harvard National Security Journal*, forthcoming.

16 Department of Justice White Paper. Available at http://msnbcmedia.msn.com/i/msnbc/sections/news/020413_DOJ_White_Paper.pdf, last accessed January 9, 2014.

17 Public Law 107–40, Authorization for Use of Military Force, available at www.gpo.gov/fdsys/pkg/PLAW-107publ40, last accessed January 9, 2014.

18 O'Connell, "The Resort to Drones": 590–1.

19 *The Caroline Case*, 1838. Available at http://avalon.law.yale.edu/19th_century/br-1842d.asp, last accessed January 9, 2014.

20 International Human Rights and Conflict Resolution Clinic at Stanford Law School and Global Justice Clinic at NYU School of Law, 2012, Living Under Drones: Death, Injury, and Trauma to Civilians from US Drone Practices in Pakistan, Stanford/NYU. Available at http://livingunderdrones.org/report/, last accessed January 13, 2014.

21 Russell Christopher, 2012, "Imminence in Justified Targeted Killing," in Claire Oakes Finkelstein, Jens David Ohlin, and Andrew Altman (eds), *Targeted Killing*, Oxford: Oxford University Press, pp. 253–84; 284.

22 Harold Koh, "The Obama Administration and International Law."

23 Jane Mayer, "Torture and Obama's Drone Program," *New Yorker*, February 15, 2013.

24 Another legal question, sidestepped by Koh in his ASIL remarks, deals with the legality of strikes in a country other than one against which the US is at war. This question has received considerable treatment (see, for example, O'Connell, 2010–11, "Remarks: The Resort to Drones under International Law"). We

have therefore concentrated our analysis on the questions of
proportionality and distinction.

25 Koh, "The Obama Administration and International Law."
26 Judith Gail Gardam, "Proportionality and Force in International
    Law," *American Journal of International Law* 87(3) (1993):
    391–413.
27 Simon Chesterman, 2001, *Just War or Just Peace? Humanitarian
    Intervention and International Law*, Oxford University Press,
    p. 10.
28 International Committee of the Red Cross, 2004, "What is
    International Humanitarian Law?," Legal Fact Sheet, Advisory
    Service on International Humanitarian Law.
29 Selections from this section have been republished from Sarah
    Kreps and John Kaag, "The Use of Unmanned Aerial Vehicles in
    Asymmetric Conflict." *Polity* 44 (2012): 260–85.
30 It should be noted that even though the United States has
    not ratified AP I, the principles embedded in it are generally
    considered customary law. See Jean-Marie Henckaerts
    and Louise Doswald-Beck, 2009, *Customary International
    Humanitarian Law*, ICRC and Cambridge University Press, Vol.
    I, p. 51.
31 Common Article 3 of the Geneva Conventions. Available at www.
    icrc.org/ihl.nsf/WebART/375–590006, last accessed January 9,
    2014.
32 International Committee of the Red Cross, "Convention (III)
    Relative to the Treatment of Prisoners of War," *International
    Humanitarian Law – Treaties and Documents*, 1949. Available at
    www.icrc.org/, last accessed January 9, 2014.
33 Article 50 of the Additional Protocol defines a civilian as "any
    person who does not belong to one of the categories of persons
    referred to in Article 4 A of the Third Convention."
34 Stathis Kalyvas, 2006, *The Logic of Violence in Civil War*, New
    York: Cambridge University Press.
35 Anisseh can Engeland, 2010, *Civilian or Combatant? A Challenge
    for the 21st Century*, New York: OUP; Thomas Bogar, "Unlawful
    Combatant or Innocent Civilian? A Call to Change the Current
    Means for Determining Status of Prisoners in the Global War on
    Terror," *Florida Journal of International Law* 21(2) (April 2009):
    29–92.
36 ICRC, "Interpretive Guidance on the Notion of Direct

Participation in Hostilities under IHL," *International Review of the Red Cross* 90(872) (Dec. 2008): 991, 1047.

37 Summary of Israeli Supreme Court Ruling on Targeted Killings, December 14, 2006; HCJ 769/02 *The Public Committee against Torture in Israel v. The Government of Israel.*

38 Combatants can exploit the intermingling of contemporary conflict environments and launch weapons from densely populated areas in order to provoke return fire that kills civilians and elicits international condemnation. See, for example, Sarah Kreps, "The Second Lebanon War: Lessons Learned," *Parameters* (Spring 2007): 72–84.

39 Customary International Humanitarian Law, March 2005, Henckaerts and Doswald-Beck, *Customary International Humanitarian Law*, p. xxxv.

40 ICRC, "Interpretive Guidance on the Notion of Direct Participation in Hostilities under IHL," *International Review of the Red Cross* 0(872) (Dec. 2008): 991–1047; 1021.

41 "Direct Participation in Hostilities: Questions and Answers." Available at www.icrc.org/eng/resources/documents/faq/direct-participation-ihl-faq-020609.htm, last accessed January 9, 2014.

42 Ibid.

43 Jens David Ohlin, 2012, "Targeting Co-Belligerents," in *Targeted Killings: Law and Morality in an Asymmetrical World*, New York: Oxford University Press, p. 68.

44 William J. Fenrick, "The *Targeted Killings* Judgment and the Scope of Direct Participation in Hostilities," *Journal of International Criminal Law* 5(2) (2007): 332–8.

45 Ohlin, "Targeting Co-Belligerents," p. 69.

46 Divergent answers to these questions can be found in Michael Gross, 2009, *Moral Dilemmas of Modern War: Torture, Assassination, and Blackmail in an Age of Asymmetric Conflict*, Cambridge University Press; and Stephen Rockel and Rick Halpern, 2009, *Inventing Collateral Damage: Civilian Casualties, War, and Empire*, Toronto: Between the Lines.

47 Yoram Dinstein, 2004, *The Conduct of Hostilities under the Law of International Armed Conflict*, Cambridge University Press.

48 Tami Davis Biddle, 2004, *Rhetoric and Reality in Air Warfare: The Evolution of British and American Ideas about Strategic Bombing, 1914–1945*, Princeton, NJ: Princeton University Press.

49 Ronald Schaffer, *Wings of Judgement: American Bombing in World War II*, Oxford University Press.

50 Inis Claude Jr, "Collective Legitimization as a Political Function of the United Nations," *International Organization* 20: 367–79; Kenneth Abbott and Duncan Snidal, *Hard and Soft Law in International Governance* (International Organization) 53(3) (2000): 421–56.

51 Dinstein, *The Conduct of Hostilities*, p. 84.

52 Antonio Cassese, 2001, *International Law*, Oxford: Oxford University Press.

53 David Bellavia and John Bruning, 2007, *House to House*, New York: Free Press, p. 10.

54 Noel Sharkey, "America's Mindless Killer Robots Must be Stopped," *The Guardian*, December 3, 2012.

55 Prosecutor of the International Criminal Court *Luis Moreno-Ocampo, "Letters to Senders regarding Iraq,"* February 9, 2006.

56 Emphasis added. USAF Targeting Intelligence Guide. Pamphlet 14–210, p. 180. Cited in Sarah Kreps and John Kaag, "The Use of Unmanned Aerial Vehicles in Asymmetric Conflict." *Polity* 44 (2012): 260–85.

57 Emphasis added. Joint Publication 1–02, Department of Defense Dictionary of Military and Associated Terms, May 30, 2008. Cited in Sarah Kreps and John Kaag, "The Use of Unmanned Aerial Vehicles in Asymmetric Conflict."

58 Selections from this section have been republished from Sarah Kreps and John Kaag, "The Use of Unmanned Aerial Vehicles in Asymmetric Conflict."

59 Additional Protocol I, 1977; Part IV: Civilian Population.

60 Prosecutor of the International Criminal Court, *Luis Moreno-Ocampo*. As with AP I, the United States is not a party to the Rome Statute, although it came into force on July 1, 2002.

61 Chris Jenks, "Law from Above: Unmanned Aerial Systems, Use of Force, and the Law of Armed Conflict," *North Dakota Law Review* 85 (2010): 649–71.

62 Avery Plaw, 2012, table 1, in *Killing by Remote Control: The Ethics of an Unmanned Military*, Oxford University Press.

63 Daniel Byman, "Why Drones Work: The Case for Washington's Weapon of Choice," *Foreign Affairs* (July/August 2013): 32–43.

64 Avery Plaw, "Counting the Dead," in Bradley Jay Strawser (ed.), *Killing by Remote Control: The Ethics of an Unmanned Military*,

New York: Oxford University Press, Kindle Edition. (Kindle Locations 2628–9).

65 David Kilcullen and Andrew Exum, "Death from Above, Outrage from Below," *New York Times*, May 16, 2009.

66 Mary Ellen O'Connell, "Unlawful Killing with Combat Drones: A Case Study of Pakistan, 2004–2009," *Notre Dame Law School Legal Studies Research Paper*, pp. 9–43, 20.

67 Avery Plaw, "Counting the Dead: Proportionality of Predation in Pakistan," in Bradley Jay Strawser (ed.), *Killing by Remote Control: The Ethics of an Unmanned Military*, New York: Oxford University Press. Kindle Edition. (Kindle Locations 2628–).

68 Michael Walzer, 2006, *Just and Unjust Wars: A Moral Argument with Historical Illustrations*, New York: Basic Books, p. 119.

69 Scott Wilson and Al Kamen, "Global War on Terror is Given a New Name," *Washington Post*, March 24, 2009.

70 A growing number of observers has noted similarities between Obama and his predecessor's approach, notwithstanding name changes. See, for example, Sarah Kreps, "American Grand Strategy after Iraq," *Orbis* 53(4) (Autumn 2009): 629–45; Charlie Savage, "Obama's War on Terror May Resemble Bush's in Some Ways," *New York Times*, February 17, 2009.

71 Mark Mazzeti, Eric Schmitt, and Robert F. Worth, "Two-Year Manhunt Led to Killing of Awlaki in Yemen," *New York Times*, September 30, 2011.

72 Walzer, *Just and Unjust Wars*, p. 120.

73 Ibid.

74 Walzer, *Just and Unjust Wars*, p. 157.

75 Walzer notes the inverse of this practice in the Vietnam War, in which the United States used indiscriminate force to minimize US casualties. *Just and Unjust Wars*, p. 188.

76 For more on radical responsibility and the risks associated with military ethics, see Walzer, *Just and Unjust Wars*, pp. 156–7. See also Michael Walzer, "The Triumph of Just War Theory – The Danger of Success," *Social Research* 69(4) (2002): 925–44.

77 Avishai Margalit and Michael Walzer, "Israel: Civilians and Combatants," *The New York Review of Books*, May 14, 2009.

78 Asa Kasher and Amos Yadlin, "Assassination and Preventive Killing," *SAIS Review* 25(1) (Winter–Spring 2005): 41–57; 51.

79 US Army, 2006, *Counterinsurgency*, Ft. Leavenworth: Army Field Manual.

80 *Counterinsurgency*, ch. 1.
81 Donald MacKenzie and Judy Wajcman, 1999, *The Social Shaping of Technology*, Open University Press; Langdon Winner, "Do Artifacts have Politics?" *Daedalus* 109(1) (Winter 1980): 121–36.

CHAPTER 5   THE ETHICS OF DRONE WARFARE

1 Sarah Kreps and John Kaag, "The Use of Unmanned Aerial Vehicles in Asymmetric Conflict," *Polity* 44 (2012): 260–85; Robert Sparrow, "Building a Better WarBot: Ethical Issues in the Design of Unmanned Systems for Military Applications," *Science and Engineering Ethics* 15(2) (2009): 169–87; Ronald Arkin, "Governing Legal Behavior: Embedding Ethics in a Hybrid Deliberative/Reactive Robot architecture," GVU Technical Report GIT-GVU-07–11; College of Computing, Georgia Tech. (2007). Bradley Strawser, "Moral Predators: The Duty to Employ Uninhabited Aerial Vehicles," *Journal of Military Ethics* 9(4) (2010): 342–68. For a detailed analysis of the relationship between ethics and technological know-how, please see John Kaag and Whitely Kaufman, "Military Frameworks: Technological Know-how and the Legitimation of Modern Warfare," *Cambridge Review of International Affairs* 22(4) (2009): 585–606.
2 Selections from this section were republished from John Kaag and Sarah Kreps, "The Moral Hazard of Drones," *New York Times*, July 23, 2012; John Kaag, "Drones, Ethics and the Armchair Soldier," *New York Times*, March 17, 2013.
3 For an elaboration of this point, please see J. Carl Ficarrotta, 2010, *Kantian Thinking About Military Ethics*, London: Ashgate.
4 Paul Kahn, "The Paradox of Riskless War," *Philosophy and Public Policy Quarterly* 22(3) (2002): 2–8.
5 Plato, 1897, *The Republic*, trans. Herbert Warren, New York: Macmillan, p. 192.
6 Plato, 1888, *The Republic*, trans. Benjamin Jowlett, Book II, 358d–61d.
7 Bradley J. Strawser has edited a collection that presents most of the central questions concerning the ethics of drone warfare. See *Killing by Remote Control*, 2012, ed. Bradley Jay Strawser, New York: Oxford University Press.

8   Leon Panetta cited in "US airstrikes in Pakistan called 'very effective,'" *CNN*, May 18, 2009.

9   Cited in John Kaag and Sarah Kreps, "The Moral Hazard of Drones," *New York Times*, July 23, 2012.

10 Selections of this section were republished from John Kaag, "Drones, Ethics and the Armchair Soldier," *New York Times*, March 17, 2013.

11 Jacoby Carter, "Just/New War Theory: Non-State Actors in Asymmetric Conflicts," *Philosophy in the Contemporary World* (Fall 2009) 16(2): 1–11.

12 Cited in Klem Ryan, "What is Wrong With Drones," in Matthew Evangelista and Henry Shue (eds), *The American Way of Bombing: How Legal and Ethical Norms Change*, forthcoming; D. Muñoz-Rojas, and J.-J. Frésard, 2004, *The Roots of Behaviour: Understanding and Preventing IHL Violations*, Geneva: International Committee of the Red Cross.

13 See Matthew Power, "Confessions of a Drone Warrior," *GQ*, October 23, 2013.

14 Thomas Hobbes, 1996, *Leviathan*, Oxford: Oxford University Press, p. 367.

15 "Report: High Levels of 'Burnout' in US Drone Pilots," National Public Radio. Rachel Martin, December 18, 2011.

16 Robert Sparrow, "Building a Better WarBot: Ethical Issues in the Design of Unmanned Systems for Military Applications," *Science and Engineering Ethics* 15(2) (2009): 169–87; Robert Sparrow, 2012, "War without Virtue?" in Bradley Jay Strawser (ed.), *Killing by Remote Control: The Ethics of an Unmanned Military*, New York: Oxford University Press. See also Edward Luttwak, "'Post Heroic Warfare' and Its Implications." Available at www.nids. go.jp/english/event/symposium/pdf/1999/sympo_e1999_5. pdf, last accessed January 9, 2014. While unable to incorporate its content due to its forthcoming status, Christian Enemark's book on the ethics of drone warfare should be mentioned here. Many of the points addressed in this chapter may receive fuller treatment in Enemark's book-length treatment of the moral implications of drone technologies. See Christian Enemark, forthcoming, *Armed Drones and the Ethics of War*, New York: Routledge.

17 J. Carl Ficarrotta, 2010, *Kantian Thinking About Military Ethics*, London: Ashgate, p. 86.

18 Jeff McMahan, 2009, *Killing in War*, Oxford: Oxford University Press.

19 Jeff McMahan, "Rethinking Just War: Part II," *New York Times*, November 12, 2012.

20 Ibid.

21 Bertrand Russell, 1959, *Common Sense and Nuclear Warfare*, New York: Routledge Chapman Press.

22 Herbert Marcuse, 1982, "Some Social Implications of Modern Technology," in Andrew Arato (ed.), *Essential Frankfurt School Reader*, London: Continuum Publishing, pp. 138–62.

23 Ibid., p. 143.

24 John Kaag and Sarah Kreps, "The Moral Hazard of Drones," *New York Times*, July 23, 2012.

25 Selections from this section were republished from John Kaag and Peter Aldinger, "The Banality of Evil Revisited: The Case of Drones," *New Left Project*, March 15, 2013. Available at www.newleftproject.org/index.php/site/article_comments/ the_banality_of_evil_revisited_the_case_of_drones, last accessed January 9, 2014.

26 Cited in "Obama's Nobel Remarks," *New York Times*, December 10, 2009.

27 Milton Mayer, 1955, *They Thought They Were Free: The Germans, 1933–45*, Chicago: University of Chicago Press, p. 166.

28 Ibid.

29 Ibid.

30 Hannah Arendt, 1994, *Eichmann in Jerusalem*, New York: Penguin, p. 247.

31 Ibid., p. 288.

32 Giorgio Agamben, 2005, *State of Exception*, Chicago: University of Chicago Press.

33 Bradley Strawser, "Moral Predators: The Duty to Employ Uninhabited Aerial Vehicles," *Journal of Military Ethics* 9(4) (2010): 342–68, 346.

34 Ibid., p. 344.

35 Uwe Steinhoff, 2013, "Killing Them Safely: Extreme Asymmetry and Its Discontents," in *Killing by Remote Control: The Ethics of an Unmanned Military*, Oxford University Press.

36 Bradley Strawser, "Moral Predators."

37 Rebecca Johnson, "The Wizard of Oz Goes to War: Unmanned

Systems in Counterinsurgency", in *Killing by Remote Control: The Ethics of an Unmanned Military*, Oxford University Press, p. 350.

38 Bradley Strawser, "Moral Predators," p. 348.

39 Avishai Margalit and Michael Walzer, "Israel: Civilians and Combatants," *The New York Review of Books*, May 14, 2009.

40 Jacoby Carter, "Just/New War Theory: Non-State Actors in Asymmetric Conflicts," *Philosophy in the Contemporary World*, (Fall 2009) 16(2): 1–11. See also Susy Killmister, "Remote Weaponry: The Ethical Implications," *Journal of Applied Philosophy* 25(2) (2008): 121–33.

41 Steven Levine, "Drones Threaten Democratic Accountability," *Three Quarks Daily*. Peter W. Singer, "Do Drones Undermine Democracy?" *New York Times*, January 21, 2012.

42 Steven Levine, "Drones Threaten Democratic Accountability."

43 These points were developed more fully in Sarah Kreps and John Kaag, "The Use of Unmanned Aerial Vehicles in Asymmetric Conflict," *Polity* 44 (2012): 260–85. Excerpts from this article appear below.

44 These points were developed elsewhere in John Kaag and Whitely Kaufman, "Military Frameworks: Technological Know-how and the Legitimation of Modern Warfare," *Cambridge Review of International Affairs* 22(4) (2009): 585–606; John Kaag, "Another Question Concerning Technology: The Ethical Implications of Homeland Defense and Security Technologies," *Homeland Security Affairs* 4(1) (2008).

45 Hilary Putnam, 2002, *The Collapse of the Fact/Value Dichotomy and Other Essays*, Cambridge, MA and London: Harvard University Press, p. 103.

46 Bradley Strawser, "Moral Predators: The Duty to Employ Uninhabited Aerial Vehicles," *Journal of Military Ethics* 9(4) (2010): 342–68.

47 US Department of Defense. News transcript, "DoD News Briefing," March 28, 2003. Available at www.defense.gov/transcripts/transcript.aspx?transcriptid=2180.

CHAPTER 6   CONCLUSION: THE WAY AHEAD

1 "President Speaks on War Effort to Citadel Cadets," *Whitehouse.gov*, Remarks by the President, December 2001.

2 Mueller 1973; Scott Gartner, "The Multiple Effects of Casualties on Public Support for War: An Experimental Approach," *American Political Science Review* 102(1) (February 2008): 95–106.

3 Joint Doctrine Note 2/11. The UK Approach to Unmanned Aircraft Systems, UK Ministry of Defence, 2011, pp. 5–8. Available at http://dronewarsuk.files.wordpress.com/2011/04/uk-approach-to-uav.pdf, last accessed January 9, 2014.

4 Quoted in Daniel Markey, "A New Drone Deal for Pakistan," *Foreign Affairs*, July 16, 2013.

5 Suzanna Koster, "Drone Wars: Pakistan Tacitly Allows Drones to Strike," *Global Post*, October 10, 2011.

6 *The Caroline Case*, 1838. Available at http://avalon.law.yale.edu/19th_century/br-1842d.asp, last accessed January 9, 2014.

7 "Reforming US Drone Strike Policies," Council Special Report no. 65. Available at www.cfr.org/wars-and-warfare/reforming-us-drone-strike-policies/p29736?co=C009601, last accessed January 13, 2014.

8 Robert Sparrow, "Building a Better WarBot: Ethical Issues in the Design of Unmanned Systems for Military Applications," *Science and Engineering Ethics* 15(2) (2009): 169–87; also Robert Sparrow, 2012, "War without Virtue?" in Bradley Jay Strawser (ed.), *Killing by Remote Control: The Ethics of an Unmanned Military*, New York: Oxford University Press.

9 Jennifer Rizzo, "Drones Soar in US Plans for Aircraft Purchases," *CNN* (June 2011).

10 Scott Peterson, "Downed US Drone: How Iran Caught the Beast." *Christian Science Monitor*, December 9, 2011. Available at www.csmonitor.com/World/Middle-East/2011/1209/Downed-US-drone-How-Iran-caught-the-beast, last accessed January 9, 2014.

11 Andrea Gilli and Mauro Gilli, "Attack of the Drones: Should we Fear the Proliferation of Unmanned Aerial Vehicles?" Paper presented for the 2013 American Political Science Association meeting, p. 21.

12 *Improvements Needed to Better Control Technology for Cruise Missiles and Unmanned Aerial Vehicles*, Government Accountability Office, 2004, p. 10.

13 I thank Navy Captain William Parker for making this point.

14 Debra Werner, "Drone Swarm: Networks of Small UAVs Offer Big Capabilities," *Defense News*, June 12, 2013.

15 I thank Colonel Patrick Mahaney, US Army, for making this point.

16 Shawn Brimley, Ben Fitzgerald, and Ely Ratner, "The Drone War Goes to Asia," *Foreign Policy, Foreign Policy*, September 17, 2013.

17 Peter Singer, "The Global Swarm," *Foreign Policy*, March 11, 2013.

18 Micah Zenko, "Reforming US Drone Strike Policies."

19 Shawn Brimley et al., "The Drone War Comes to China," *Foreign Policy*, September 17, 2013.

20 "US Looks to Export Drone Technology to Allies," *Reuters*, March 25, 2010.

21 The United States sells drones to other countries, but has limited those sales to reconnaissance. For example, it is exporting Predators to the United Arab Emirates, but the drones are unarmed. See "UAE to Buy US-Made Drones in Military Expansion," *Fox News*, February 19, 2013.

22 "Israel Tops US in Drone Exports," *Dayton Business Journal*, May 20, 2013.

23 Tia Goldenberg, "Israel Leads Global Drone Exports as Demand Grows," *Associated Press*, June 5, 2013.

24 Micah Zenko, "Reforming US Drone Strike Policies."

25 Andrew Winner, "The Proliferation Security Initiative: The New Face of Interdiction," *Washington Quarterly* 28(2) (Spring 2005): 129–43.

26 Gerald Dworkin, "Is More Choice Better than Less?" *Midwest Studies in Philosophy* 7(1) (1982): 56.

27 G. John Ikenberry, 2001, *After Victory: Institutions, Strategic Restraint, and the Rebuilding of Order after Wars*, Princeton University Press, pp. 1–2.

28 Ikenberry, *After Victory*, pp. 1–13, 16

Index

counterterrorism, 160n27
international law, 16, 84–5,
    86, 103
killing of al-Awlaki in, 30, 69,
    98
lack of Congressional
    approval, 66

number of drone strikes in, 4,
    28–30
public opinion in, 46, 47

Zegart, Amy, 68
Zenko, Micah, 8–9, 49, 67–8,
    142–3, 145, 151, 155